—THE—
THURSDAY
SPEECHES

Lessons in Life, Leadership, and Football
from Coach Don James

Peter Tormey, Ph.D.

The Thursday Speeches
Lessons in Life, Leadership, and Football from Coach Don James

By Peter Tormey © Copyright 2014

ISBN: 978-0-692-32835-4

Cover design: Matt Gollnick
Page layout: Lighthouse24

Contents

PART II: THEMES OF THE THURSDAY SPEECHES

PART III: GLIMMERS

PART IV: A LASTING LEGACY

—Dedication—

This book is dedicated to the late and legendary University of Washington football Coach Don James and his family. James' words and leadership have inspired the best in the countless people whose lives he touched, including mine, during the four years he was my coach at Washington.

The Thursday Speeches represents an appreciative tribute to a great man. I hope this book will allow many others to benefit from the wisdom of Don James, a giant of college football and a person of humility, faith, and love.

Whether in athletics, business, government, or in the context of one's own family, the best leaders inspire others to harness their utmost potential to benefit the common good. No one did that as well as Don James.

I also dedicate this book to my wife Kelly for her never-ending love and support, and to our children Mary Kate, Tara, and Brendan that they may live inspired lives.

—Acknowledgements—

This book would not have been possible without the assistance and time of Don James, my football coach at the University of Washington (1976–1979) whose leadership I will never forget.

Don believed strongly in the power of education to transform lives. He believed education was a lifelong process and, as *The Thursday Speeches* demonstrates, he was a voracious reader who was constantly learning and looking for creative new ways to improve the Husky football program. Lifelong learning, he told me, was the single thing that helped him most in his career.

"The key thing is you never stop learning," he said. "You are looking to learn every day."

Throughout his exceptional career, Coach James helped every student who sought his assistance in an educational project—whether it was a quick interview with a reporter for the student newspaper or—in my case—a request for his active participation in a doctoral dissertation that involved multiple interviews over the course of several years.

Don urged us, his players, to go as far as we possibly could with education. I took his advice and earned a Ph.D. I hope this book inspires you to seize the power of learning to realize your dreams and make a difference for others in our world.

Special thanks to Carol James for her support of this project. Grateful appreciation also to editor Linda Nathan, Logos Word Designs, LLC, www.logosword.com; Doug Heatherly, Lighthouse24, for interior page design and formatting; and Jeff Harrison for his advice and recommendations. Acknowledgements are also due to Rev. Robert H. Schuller, sportswriter Steve Rudman, and the estate of author Og Mandino for permission to quote.

A portion of the proceeds from the book will be contributed to the UW's Don James Football Endowment Fund to provide scholarship assistance to student-athletes who participate in the Husky football program.

—Introduction—

Two days before Christmas 1974, Don James seized the reins of a University of Washington football program in disarray. In his 18 years at Washington, James compiled a 153-57-2 record en route to becoming the most successful football coach in the history of UW and the Pacific-12 Conference. He took his teams to 15 bowl games (10-5) including nine straight from 1979-87. He guided the Huskies to six Rose Bowls and is one of only four coaches to win four Rose Bowl games. His 1991 team finished the season 12-0, beat Michigan in the Rose Bowl, and was named National Champion by *USA Today*/CNN, UPI, the Football Writers, *Sports Illustrated,* and several computer rankings. President of the American Football Coaches Association in 1989, James was National College Coach of the Year twice. He was inducted into the Husky Hall of Fame in 1993 and entered the College Football Hall of Fame in 1997. As but one measure of his coaching skill, *Sports Illustrated* once named the three best college football coaches in the country: No. 1, Don James; No. 2, Don James; No. 3, Don James.

As a player in James' second recruiting class at Washington, I was fortunate to have been part of what James would later describe as "the cornerstone" of his program. In summer training camp before my freshman season, Coach James told us we were there to fulfill our destiny, to be a part of something great, to play in the Rose Bowl and, importantly, to win it. We believed him and it came to pass.

Under James' leadership, our teams beat Michigan in the 1978 Rose Bowl and Texas in the 1979 Sun Bowl, and he helped establish

Washington as a perennial powerhouse for nearly two decades. With James as our coach, we knew we had a chance to beat any team, any day.

Although Coach James died of pancreatic cancer on October 20, 2013 at age 80, his legacy and wisdom live on through the countless lives he touched and changed. His life was based on strong values, faith, and an unmatched work ethic he learned as a child growing up in Massillon, Ohio, during the Great Depression, one of four sons of Florence and Thomas James. Don's father held two jobs to ensure that the James boys could go to college, working from midnight until 8 a.m. at the steel mill before turning around and laying brick for another eight hours, every day, five days a week. For his part, Don began carrying bricks for pay at age 9 in the summer for his uncle's construction company. In doing so, he began to realize that a college education would be one key to his future success; he was already familiar with the other key: hard work.

He played quarterback and defensive back for two state championship teams at Massillon High, idolized his coaches, and decided then and there to become a football coach. He went on to play quarterback at the University of Miami where he set five school passing records and married the love of his life, Carol Hoobler.

At Washington, Coach James used words and stories to motivate the Huskies to slay the football giants of his day. This book pulls back the curtain to give readers an insider's perspective to the exact words James used to inspire the Huskies to reach the pinnacle of American college football. His words, the basis for *The Thursday Speeches,* offer valuable advice for everyone living in our competitive world, especially coaches, athletes, and leaders in all fields of endeavor.

The Thursday Speeches

James wrote his pre-game speeches by longhand each Wednesday, before practice, on 11-by-14-inch yellow legal pads while sitting at his office desk. He made final edits each Thursday before taking the final speech with him into the room where the Huskies were gathered before practice, placing the pages on a podium and reciting them—often with great passion—to his teams for 18 seasons. The speeches offer a portal to James' success—revealing the words he used to inspire the Huskies to victory and direct them to visualize success during the two days leading up to kickoff, which he called the "final 48 hours."

Upon my request, Coach James provided me with the majority of his Thursday speeches to use as the basis for my doctoral dissertation, which I completed and published in 2007. I studied all of the speeches he provided to me and completely transcribed more than 100 of the best. This book contains excerpts—and in some cases most or all of the text—from approximately 55 of his best Thursday speeches. Coach James had encouraged me to publish this book, and his memorial service at UW in October 2013 inspired me to finish it. I was saddened when he died that I did not have the opportunity to tell him the tremendous influence he had on my life. I felt compelled to finish this book—both as a lasting tribute to a great man and as a permanent source of inspiration and benefit to others now and in the future.

The Power of Language in Leadership

Communication scholar Klaus Krippendorff (1995) examined the ways that great leaders employ language to construct a new version of reality for their followers. The late French philosopher and scholar Michel Foucault (1979) suggested power is "exercised rather than possessed"; Krippendorff took this a step further to point out the indisputable relationship of language to power: "Power is exercised rather than possessed, by someone and in words." James' transformation of the UW program proves what Krippendorff theorized: Leaders who are skilled using language have the power to literally speak things into being. *The Thursday Speeches* shows this is precisely what Coach James did.

The Final 48 Hours

Most college football coaches deliver their major pre-game motivational speeches to their teams on Fridays, 24 hours or less before kickoff. Don James, however, was convinced from his first days at Washington that the ideal time for his big talk to his teams was before practice on Thursdays, (approximately) 48 hours before kickoff. James believed that setting a team's focused mental preparation on Thursday gave players an extra 24 hours to process his strategic directions and visualize themselves in game situations.

James learned about the concept of the final 48 hours as an assistant at Florida State to head Coach Bill Peterson—James' first job as a full-time assistant coach in college. Peterson was one of the first college football coaches in the country to focus players' attention 48 hours before games. At that time, in the mid-1950s, some coaches encouraged mental preparation but most spoke to their teams on Fridays.

"Basically for everybody I had worked with or played with it was always the day before, 24 hours before," James said. "Bill Peterson was part of the group that included (former Louisiana State University Coach Paul) Dietzel, (San Diego Chargers Coach Sid) Gillman and (legendary Alabama Coach Paul "Bear") Bryant who said, 'We're going to start the mental approach 48 hours before the game.' Bill got us going and we did that for six years with Bill at Florida State."

Recognizing the advantage of starting his teams' mental focus early, James studied and continued to develop his approach to the final 48 hours throughout his career. He taught the Huskies to visualize themselves making plays hundreds of times during the final 48 hours—in many situations. James believed strongly that this prepared players to free-flow, react intuitively and play better. Always an innovator, James' development of the final 48 hours became a signature of his success.

James said he first began to consider the impacts of mental preparation as a high school football player.

"A lot of my coaches over the years had talked about mental preparation. I can remember them saying 'just feel the grip of the ball, the leather and smell the grass.' They would talk about 'seeing yourself play, feeling yourself out there playing, throwing and catching. You can be the projector; like being in the press box, watch yourself play.' There are a lot of psychologists today who think they just invented this," he said.

As a highly sought-after defensive coordinator, James brought the final 48 hours approach to Coach Chalmers W. "Bump" Elliott at Michigan and Coach Eddie Crowder at Colorado.

"At Michigan, Bump was a Friday guy. I said, 'Bump, this is what I used to do and what I learned from Dietzel and Sid Gillman and all those guys' and he started it and did it the two years I was at Michigan, he really liked it. Then I went to Colorado and Eddie Crowder was the same way, a Friday guy, and so I explained the same basic concept and so he started it and liked it. It was a matter of kicking the mental part of game preparation in another 24 hours earlier and getting the guys to try to realize how important these hours are before the game and that this is the time to start to get serious."

James' success at Washington is attributable in large measure to his extraordinary communication skills, and his ability to direct and focus players' mental preparation during the final 48 hours. James' Thursday speeches formally began the final 48 hours and put players on notice that their demeanor had better reflect the urgency of the upcoming game.

James' Rx for the Huskies' Success

The Thursday speeches were the delivery devices for James' potent pre-game mental medicine. The speeches urge players to devote themselves to the final 48 hours—seeing themselves delivering devastating tackles, throwing pinpoint passes, running to daylight, and changing a game's tempo with a bone-crushing block.

In addition to instructing the Huskies on how to use visualization to play their best on game day, James used the Thursday speeches to help players achieve what he called "competitive greatness," and to emphasize the importance of maintaining a positive outlook regardless of adversity. Finally, Coach James used his Thursday speeches to impart wisdom and fatherly life lessons to generations of young men.

In the first part of each Thursday speech, James read through a series of quantitative measures of the Huskies' season performance to date based on team goals. In the second part of the speech, he identified an opponent's key strengths and weaknesses. The final part contained the motivational and persuasive strategies James employed to direct the Huskies to victory. Many of the speeches in this book are excerpts drawn solely from the final part of his talks.

Immediately following each Thursday speech, James led the team to Husky Stadium for a short, crisp practice in sweats, focused on last-minute mental checks, awareness of trick plays, and substitutions in multiple scenarios. For home games, the top 50 or so players departed from Husky Stadium on Friday afternoon for a hotel across Lake Washington in Bellevue, after taking written tests to ensure they knew the game-plan. At the hotel, we gathered for even more mental preparedness drills before continuing our individual visualization efforts as the clock ticked toward Saturday's kickoff.

James told me he tried to accomplish three things with the Thursday speeches: inspire players, get them to rest, and to perform the mental preparation work he prescribed.

"There is a time when you've got to get better mentally. That was always the approach. You just get guys focused. You know if you play in the offensive line, you've got all these plays and check-offs and defenses stunting and shifting there is so much to it that you've really got to spend a lot of time on it and there is no way you can run enough plays. You can't run everything (in practice) to prepare for it," James said. "Well, if I know what I'm doing and I know the steps and I know the footwork and I know whom to block, I can do the job—regardless of what they do. What that does is give you confidence. How are you going to beat somebody good without confidence? This was a way we could do that."

Of course, no speech could ever guarantee a win, and some of his most stirring Thursday speeches did not result in victories, particularly during his first few years at Washington. However, the speeches built upon each other to transform the Huskies' thinking and performance. James' belief in the importance of the Thursday speeches grew throughout his career. He put so much time, thought, and energy into these speeches because he experienced their effectiveness.

Through the Thursday speeches, James invited his players and coaches to join him and dedicate ourselves completely to the shared dream of excellence. The speeches persuaded us to do the excruciating work necessary to make that vision become reality.

Author's Note: The speeches printed in this book have been transcribed directly from Coach James' handwritten legal pads and, as a result, may not be grammatically or stylistically correct in all cases; his capitalizations are retained. Longer blocks of the Thursday speeches are indented for easier reading, as are longer quotes from interviews with James, and longer quotes from others in the final section, "Lasting Legacy."

Part I

GETTING TO
THE ROSE BOWL

— 1975 —

Setting Goals, Changing Attitudes

Soon after taking over as head coach at Washington, Don James met with the players, including three dozen seniors, and challenged them to commit to going to a bowl game in his first season. At that time, the Rose Bowl was the only postseason bowl possible for Washington. To get there, Washington had to win the Pacific-8 Conference championship. Some of the players scoffed at James' suggestion, reminding him the Huskies hadn't been to the Rose Bowl since 1963, and their last winning season was 1972. James stuck to the goal and it made all the difference.

The objective—so bold, so outrageous, and so unrealistic—shocked the players and became a mantra that would catalyze the program's rise from mediocrity to a national power. While it would take the Huskies three years to reach the Rose Bowl and win it, James' goal—mentioned in one of his first meetings with the players and reiterated often in his Thursday speeches—set in motion a long chain of events culminating in the 1991 national championship.

"This blew a lot of our people's minds right when I got there, when I started saying 'we're going to have a bowl-season philosophy.' In those days there wasn't anybody going to any bowls from Washington. I said, 'No we're going to have a philosophy of how we are going to approach a bowl.' And the word got out," he said.

College football programs do not become powerhouses overnight. Jim Owens, Washington's head coach from 1957 to 1974, led Washington to three Rose Bowls in the 1960s, winning two. But by the early-1970s, the thrill was gone. The civil rights movement and campus protests over America's involvement in the Vietnam War were changing the culture of college campuses, even in athletics. Old ways of doing things were no longer effective. Owens led the Huskies to 10-1 (overall) seasons in 1959 and 1960, and the conference championship and Rose Bowl victories each year. The Huskies won an additional conference championship, in 1963, but lost the Rose Bowl, and had mixed success in the 11 seasons since: re-cording five winning seasons, two even seasons, and four losing campaigns.

By mid-August of 1975, as James presided over his first two-a-day pre-season workouts at Washington, he had heard some of the Huskies' grumblings. James had seen this before, at Kent State where he turned around the program before coming to Washington. He realized that transforming Washington football would take focused leadership, clear goals, sacrifice from everyone involved, and some wins to convince the skeptics. While some of the skepticism played out in the media and in public, James was most concerned with the team's attitude.

He had to make the players believe. It was the only way they would make the incredible sacrifices necessary to achieve his goals. He told the players before pre-season two-a-day workouts that the drills would be so difficult some of them would quit. James said he wanted players with a positive attitude, those who could commit to do the "awful" hard work necessary to win.

As he discovered, transforming the program would be more like turning around an aircraft carrier than a speedboat. For the players to believe James' promise to lift Washington to glory, they had to see some return on their investment of blood, sweat, and pain.

The Huskies had to win some games.

To win, James knew he had to persuade players that his plan was sound and worthy of their commitment. For that critical work, James relied on his Thursday speeches, his direction to his assistants, and their follow-up talks to players.

In the pre-season, during two-a-day workouts, James spoke to the team in the evening—offering equal parts motivation, inspiration, and explanation. Once the season began, his Thursday speeches became his primary strategic tool to inspire and motivate the Huskies. Those experiencing their first Thursday speech saw a new side of James, an amped up intensity and competitive fierceness that struck fear in many and contrasted with his usual demeanor. James often rocked back and forth, heel to toe, at the podium before us. His speeches started slow, broad and serious, covering the itinerary and other scheduling details. As the speeches progressed, James seemed to grow more intense by the minute. His cadence quickened, his face reddened, and his eyes flashed displaying his fierce competitiveness.

As his speeches reached a crescendo, James appeared battle-ready. This Don James, the competitor, was a side of him that only his players and coaches saw—a contrast to his more reserved and affable public persona. At times filled with sound and fury, the Thursday speeches inspired players to embrace the hard work required to become champions. James' words infected us all with Husky Fever and made victory contagious.

Joe Steele, who set Washington's single-season rushing record in 1978, which stood until 1990 (when it was broken by Greg Lewis), remembers the precision in which the Thursday team meetings began.

"All players were in the meeting room at least five minutes beforehand. The door would open and the position coaches came in first. Then came

Dick Scesniak, the offensive coordinator, and then Jim Mora, the defensive coordinator. The room became very quiet. Coach James came in last, right at 3 o'clock. He would start slow, build a case for our opponent, and he would close it out in a way that would have everyone in the room all jacked up," said Steele, whose UW career rushing record, set in 1979, stood until 1994 (when it was broken by Napoleon Kaufman).

James-led Huskies Debut vs. Arizona State
September 11, 1975

For the 1975 season-opener, the Huskies traveled to face an outstanding Arizona State team led by All-Americans Mike Haynes at cornerback, Larry Gordon at linebacker, and wide receiver John Jefferson. In his first Thursday speech at Washington, James told the players and coaches they have similar jobs and must be "totally prepared," and "know the plan thoroughly."

James explained that effective pre-game preparation involves meetings, film study, practice, and "quiet-time concentration" focused on football. He warned of the dangers teams face when traveling—distraction and loss of concentration—and shared how golf legend Ben Hogan used mental visualization to succeed. Although the Huskies' difficult physical work was finished by Thursday, James told players their mental visualization work had just begun, and should occupy their minds for the next 48 hours until kickoff.

"See yourself doing your job successfully every play," he said. "As (golfer) Lee Trevino said, 'If you haven't brought it with you on game day, don't expect to find it.'"

James said he expected players to put their "game faces on" with no "entertainers."

> When we meet Friday morning up until the final whistle, I don't want any entertainers on this team. You are not expected to entertain your buddies. You don't have to make anyone laugh. No playing music, whistling or singing—when you do, you are then

disrupting team concentration. Other players break their concentration. Other players will get upset with you. We then break
the team unity factor.

James said his experience in more than twenty years of competing in
games had shown that "the more seriously a team takes a game the more
serious they will be on Thursday, Friday, and Saturday." He said, "I've
seen levity at dinner Friday night and pre-game, loud conversations that
have nothing to do with the game, and most normally I've seen horse-shit
play."

The major themes James set for the ASU game were team confidence and
team respect; both, he said, must be earned.

> This will be a hitting contest. And we must win this phase of the
> game. We need to have each man win his individual battles,
> physically kick hell out of your man. Dominate. Remember the
> enjoyment of this trip and from the game of football is No. 1
> from the game competition, and No. 2 from the feeling that
> comes with success. The return trip is the most important to en-
> joy.

At the end of his speech, James drew a large purple line—a sharp contrast
to the black ink he used for his speech. Under that purple line, he wrote in
large letters in a big purple box: CHAMPION.

Neither James nor the Huskies enjoyed the trip home from Tempe after
losing 35-12 to the Frank Kush-coached Sun Devils who finished the season
12-0 and ranked No. 2 in the nation. Led by sophomore quarterbacks
Bruce Hardy and Fred Mortensen, the Sun Devils rolled up 422 yards
in total offense while their defense held the Huskies to 260 total yards.

Next Up: The Texas Longhorns and Earl Campbell
September 18, 1975

Coach James' concepts of competitive greatness and visualizing victory
were among his most important themes and are developed in Part II of

this book. These themes appeared in this, his second Thursday speech in his first season as the Huskies prepared to host No. 8-ranked Texas, featuring a devastatingly powerful and fleet-footed sophomore back named Earl Campbell who would go on to win the 1977 Heisman Trophy.

James told the Huskies that Texas would not look past them. He reminded players of their game at Texas the previous year when the Huskies lost 21-35 to the then No. 18-ranked Longhorns. James said the Huskies held Texas in too much esteem, and reminded players that they came away from that contest feeling they should have won.

"No one in America outside this room thinks we can win," he told the Huskies. "We must believe in ourselves. Each man in here has got to feel that he can whip his Texas counterpart."

The crucible of competition could catalyze the Huskies to beat Texas, he said.

James scoured the media for material to help motivate the Huskies and found some grist for that mill in a Seattle newspaper the week before they played Texas. Quoting the newspaper, James asked the Huskies: "Do Husky players and coaches have the guts to show up this week?" He challenged the Huskies to shock the naysayers and knock Texas out of the rankings.

James instructed players to use mental visualization to "see" themselves making game-breaking plays that would stir the crowd to its feet. He urged the Huskies to continue to focus on their visualization work, winning individual battles throughout the final 48 hours. He told players their full senses should be involved in the process:

> We can't block or tackle now—no more in the Final 48 Hours. We practice for 80 minutes in sweats today; there is limited physical work time left. But you can block 80P or 48 (specific plays) 500 times between now and 1:30 Saturday. How? Mentally. You can stop Campbell on 32 & 33 or (quarterback

Marty) Akins on load (another play) 500 times before now and 1:30 Saturday. How? Mentally.

Psychologists tell us that we must close our eyes, feel the pads on. Hear the crowd noise. Hear the cracking of pads. Feel the texture of the ball—Astroturf and uniforms. Smell the odors surrounding game. Just continually focus attention on your assignment against what they will do. Visualize movement; picture yourself successfully exploding on your opponent. See yourself knocking them down and back.

In this speech, James introduced his use of the metaphor "putting on mental weight" to describe his notion that players could use the power of focused mental visualization to perform better and make themselves figuratively bigger and literally stronger.

As he told the team in his Thursday speech the week prior, James reiterated the importance of players putting on their "game face" in the final 48 hours.

Let me take you back to last Friday night and the bus ride to the stadium and return. There was 24 hours until kickoff. In the first bus, I was in the front seat. The starters, captains, seniors were in rows two to the back. I could hear you in your discussions. Not all, but many (some in back row). Not one discussion that I heard was on football. Cars. Nightclubs. Stores. Weather.

First point: A little quiet reflection on the game; you couldn't if you wanted to. Second point: That's one valuable hour taken away from mental preparation you didn't do and you prevented others. Men, I don't like to bitch at you anytime. We're a team in this together. I definitely don't like bitching in the last 48 hours, but someone has to assume some leadership around here. It's going to take some individual players speaking out, saying, "Get quiet! Don't talk to me now!" Grim determination. I've seen athletes who would refuse to see their family on game day. We've got to have a "get away from me" attitude and say, "if you're not talking about football and Texas, I don't want to talk with you."

Attitude. This is the most important thing on my mind and in my life at this time. Don't entertain people. Don't carry on idle BS conversations. Lock yourself in on your game. Many times it's the player that is in back-up role that is most relaxed. Every man must get ready.

What now? Believe in yourself. You can whip your man. Believe we can win as a team. If we believe, we will play far better as a team. Master your plan. Put on your mental weight. We've seen men much smaller than Campbell stop him in his tracks. We've also seen him run over bigger people. Measure yourself. Let your mind run rampant with mental talk about this game. What areas do you need more practice—mentally? Don't overlook any phase of your play. Kicking is extremely important. We can cause fumbles when we kick to them. If you get your man we can score when they kick to us.

Gear yourself for your best physical effort. Why are there world records? In nearly every instance it's an athlete recording his greatest effort. Competition does this, mental and physical preparation. Review your attitude about competition. In individual battles, don't let your man win any. Whether the score is even, we're ahead or behind, destroy your opponent. Develop killer instinct. When your man is beaten, put him away.

Next, James asked the Huskies to consider adopting "a temporary distaste" of Texas as a motivational tool until the game was over.

A temporary distaste for Texas, the state, the university. The team is coming in here laughing at us. Coming in here trying to fatten their national ratings at our expense. Use this to help place you in a proper emotional state.

In summary, he reminded players what a win over Texas would mean for the Huskies.

Every football fan in America will look for the score Saturday night and Sunday morning. It's the most important game on our schedule. Why? We want to win our championship. This is the type of team we must be able to whip if we are serious about our objective. They have something we want: Reputation and tradition. They have won by winning consistently; they have won by winning big. They have won by winning over good power teams. We have a great opportunity this week. If we believe—and prepare during these Final 48 Hours—we can achieve.

Earl Campbell rushed for 198 yards and three touchdowns to power Texas to a 28-10 victory. Although the Huskies' 0-2 record had yet to reflect it, James' major themes were beginning to reshape Washington football.

Clear Goals and the Story of the Cheshire Cat
September 25, 1975

After starting his first UW season at 0-2, James knew he had to beat Navy on Sept. 27 to avoid having the Midshipmen torpedo his turn-around campaign. A dangerous 2-0 Navy team would enter Husky Stadium ranked No. 20 in the nation after destroying Virginia and Connecticut. In this, his third Thursday speech to the Huskies, James incorporated what he had just learned at a UW engineering conference. Invited to speak at the conference, James arrived two hours early to hear a lecture about leadership.

"That guy made an impression on me," James told me. "He said, 'Many leaders fail to let their people know what is expected of them and where they want to go.' In other words, if you are working for me and you don't know where we are going and what I want, regardless of what you want it doesn't seem to work. His major point that I walked away with is this: If you are in a leadership role, the best thing you can do as far as productivity is let people know where you want to go."

As a result of that lecture, James developed his Pyramid of Objectives, a graphical construct that would shape the direction of Husky football. In his Thursday speech on Sept. 25, James reminded the Huskies where he was leading them, and he challenged them to do the difficult work needed to reach their goals: the conference championship and a Rose Bowl victory. In one of his more colorful talks, James employed a familiar narrative to remind the players and coaches where he was leading them. He invoked the words of the Cheshire cat from Lewis Carroll's classic novel *Alice's Adventures in Wonderland* to underscore the importance of the Huskies knowing and controlling their destiny.

> We must know where we're going at this stage. We must know what we want to accomplish, where we want to get to. This reminded me of the wisdom of the Cheshire cat in answer to Alice's question in *Alice in Wonderland*. She asks, "Would you tell me, please, which way I go from here?" The answer, of course, was, "That depends a good deal on where you want to get to," said the cat. "I don't care much where," said Alice. "Then it doesn't matter which way you go," said the cat.
>
> Men, we have got to know—and care—the direction from here. We have established crystal clear goals. The fact that you are in this room is evidence that you are willing to pay the price (awful price) to get there.
>
> Test time is drawing near again. How do we pass that test? Give football what it deserves. Give your team what it deserves. Tap your capacity. Respect yourself. Intend to succeed. There is a question that we will have to ask ourselves Sunday and then again in nine weeks when the '75 season will be over. And while we are asking ourselves this question this test will be completely recorded, filmed, taped, broadcast, and written about. That question is: "Did I give it everything that it deserves?" If you have, the rewards will always match the service.
>
> You can only grow and learn the great valuable lessons through total commitment. There are those of you in here who wish

you had been better committed during our first two weeks of preparation. Those with commitment have a special glow about them. Those that are not are fairly obvious to your peer groups and coaches. An affirmation I'll never forget: "Isn't it wonderful what can be accomplished when nobody cares who gets the credit."

James again emphasized "must"—saying the Huskies "must become a more physical team. It was a physical week—make it pay off." Then he told the Huskies they must "dedicate the game to physically kicking hell out of Navy."

James also touched on the theme of developing a healthy—albeit temporary—distaste for the opponent.

Distaste—mad—angry—bitter:
1) Because of our record 0-2;
2) Because Navy thinks they are all world;
3) Because people do not yet respect us;
4) Because we are determined to accomplish the things that only we believe and know we can do.

As the speech drew to a close, James again told the Huskies they must:

Get mentally get jacked up to be hitters. Play with reckless abandon, the definition of which is giving up natural impulses, freedom from constraint. Navy players do not fear us. Navy players do not respect us. They think there is no way they can lose, regardless of how good or bad they play. I don't know about you but I personally find it distasteful competing without respect. But we must earn it! It's not coming just handed down.

James concluded by circling back to the tale of the Cheshire cat:

"We know which way to go from here! Let's get to work!"

Defensive back Al Burleson knocked down a Navy two-point conversion attempt with 1:08 left in the game and scored on a 41-yard third-quarter pass interception to lift the Huskies to a 14-13 win.

The Huskies gained some much-needed confidence, and understood where James was leading them.

The Pyramid of Objectives Offers a Roadmap to Success

Coach James' Pyramid of Objectives would become an integral part of the Husky football playbook for players and coaches, and a key to success—serving as a visual roadmap to the Huskies' achievement. The Pyramid was constructed in such a way that short-term goals had to be achieved before long-term objectives became possible. James created the goals at the start of each season and tracked their progress weekly—giving the Huskies an update at the start of every Thursday speech. The goals became keys to victory on offense, defense, and in the kicking game. They included statistics such as total yards on offense and defense, passing yards gained and allowed, rushing yards gained and allowed, etc. James continued to shape and refine the Pyramid throughout his Husky career to motivate and measure teams. Players also used it to achieve individual goals.

Legendary former UCLA basketball Coach John Wooden created a pyramid in 1948, a character-development ladder that could be used for any goal-oriented process with each rung representing a character trait needed for success. James credited Wooden's pyramid for helping to inspire his Pyramid of Objectives.

"I had read John Wooden's book and I got (from the UW engineering lecture) the idea of telling people that work with you where you want them to go and how to get there. I could (with the Pyramid of Objectives) tell the players where I wanted to go with the program and how to get there," he said. "Everything would get you to a national championship. I redid that every year. The blocks would stay the same and I would change all the numbers based on what happened the last year in the league."

James' Pyramid of Objectives also showed each player how he could play a role in the Huskies' success.

"You just go through and circle the things that impact you. If you are a walk-on or a third-teamer, the travel team would be a goal for you. If you are a second-teamer, then maybe starting would be a goal for you. If you are a starter, then all-league would be a goal. If you are all-league, then All-American. I got the idea that this would be better to spell out to players," he said. "For instance, if you were on the kickoff coverage team and last year we were fifth, and we are just two yards off being No. 1, let's take some pride. And the position coach who was responsible for kickoff coverage could handle his guys with this objective. The position coaches handling the kicking phases would say, 'We've got to pick it up.' Or if we're leading, 'We've got to stay up there.' Or, 'We're playing the No. 1 team this week and we've got to pick it up.' So there were a lot of ways we would use the Pyramid of Objectives."

Atop James' Pyramid of Objectives were the goals of winning the conference championship, becoming Rose Bowl champions and national champions, and graduating 90 percent of all football players. Other goals sought more qualitative improvements:

- Be a great competitor.
- Become a leader.
- No fumbles or interceptions.
- Defense score or provide field position.
- Backs make tough yards.
- Quarterbacks exercise great judgment.
- Receivers block and make tough catches.
- Defense contain the run.
- Execute a Husky tackle.
- Defense produce four turnovers and prevent big gains.

The Pyramid of Objectives also freed James from a myopic view of day-to-day details to provide him with a big-picture dashboard of key indicators of the Huskies' health and progress toward their goals.

GENERAL INFORMATION - Continued

F. Pyramid Objectives:

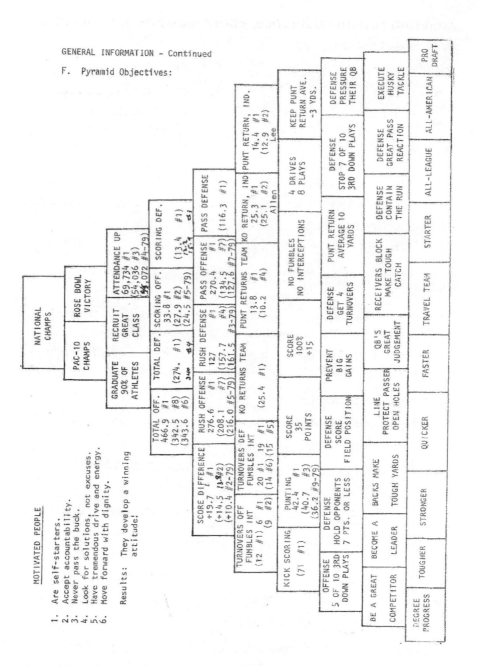

Pyramid of Objectives

Suffering Brings Endurance, Endurance Fosters Character
October 2, 1975

In his Thursday speech before the 1-2 Huskies traveled to Eugene to battle historic interstate rival Oregon, James told the players about the flurry of interest and concern about the game that he'd heard from alumni and "everyone I've come into contact with this week." James also offered a life lesson, another major theme found in his Thursday speeches—this one about the nature of suffering.

James shared the questions he'd been asked that week by concerned alumni and fans:

Are your guys up?

Are your guys ready?

Do they remember their last trip to Eugene and the 58-0 loss?

Do they remember last year's trip to the state of Oregon and the 9-23 loss to Oregon State?

Do they know this is a great rivalry?

Do they know that over the years this game has been close and has not necessarily gone true to form?

Do they know that the games have been close prior to the past two seasons?

Do they know that Oregon has had to live with the humiliating defeat (1974) for a year, 66-0, and that they have had to look at that film over and over?

Do they know that Oregon is much improved over 1974?

Do they know that all three Northwest schools feel their most important game is with Washington?

Do they know that a win will make their season and that Oregon always seems to play their best against Washington and Oregon State?

James added, "Alumni have requested appointments. People in the department have all cautioned me and most have come into my office very serious."

Pausing for dramatic impact, James offered the compelling rejoinder to all the questions he had fielded so far that week:

"My feeling is that they are questioning our intelligence—yours and mine," James said, his voice rising.

> Hell, this is our championship game. You don't play one game to win the championship. You play seven in this league. You don't play six contests and then all of a sudden everyone gets excited and says, "Hey this is our big game, it's for a title." You have to win one in order to play and have a chance at another championship game.

> Besides, all of the questions are redundant. Coaches on this staff played and coached in these Oregon games. Thirty-three seniors, some in their fifth year, have played in these games. That's why I say the questions come as an apparent indictment of our intelligence. Anyone who can't get ready to play a championship game does not belong in competitive athletics.

James then described the strengths and weaknesses of the Ducks before telling players that their 66-0 thrashing of Oregon the previous year had created tremendous doubt among the Ducks.

> They respect you. They are building their hate for us. They desperately need and want a victory. They recognize the rivalry. They have improved. We can help reinforce this doubt with early success. Regardless, prepare yourself for a 60-minute dogfight. We talked all week—emphasis—about consistency.

> Another word that crops up in football and in life is character. Player has character? Team has character? Definition? Quality, moral constitution, reputation, good respect, ethical standard.

A team with character is never upset—it develops proper respect for competition. We are favorites. Everyone will expect us to win. Eyebrows are only raised if we don't succeed.

Being judged as a team with character doesn't occur overnight—it takes time—takes that price—that awful price. We are suffering from no championship in 12 years.

James then quoted a New Testament passage to frame the link between suffering and endurance.

The Apostle Paul wrote in 1st and 2nd Corinthians: "Suffering brings endurance." Seniors were 2-9 and 5-6, are experiencing a new program, new staff, two tough losses and one tough win. Endurance brings character. Many people don't gain endurance because they don't suffer—they quit. Character brings hope; your heads are up. You want to do well, succeed. Regardless of what has happened over these past few years you still think it can be done.

People with strong character, James said, "continually strive to improve. Always do their best. Keep a bright outlook. They are committed."

So, essentially, character is a real controlling factor in man's success—helped by maturity and experience. We have suffered through hard work. In doing this we have developed endurance. Then we, through maturity and experience, are developing team character. Stop listening to doubters. Stop worrying about how mad Oregon is. Instead, each man concern himself with his individual plan and this team will prove what we believe and know we can do.

Sophomore transfer quarterback Warren Moon scored on a 1-yard plunge late in the third quarter to secure the Huskies' 27-17 victory. Washington improved to 2-2 and prepared to travel to Tuscaloosa the following week to take on the No. 7-ranked Alabama and its iconic leader, Coach Paul "Bear" Bryant in his 18th season leading the Crimson Tide.

The Tide Rolls and Changes Everything

Everything changed the following Saturday, Oct. 11, when the Crimson Tide stormed Washington like a tsunami, drowning the Huskies 52-0 with wave after crashing wave of power, strength, speed and quickness—handing James one of the worst, most humiliating defeats of his career.

Playing the Huskies for the first time since the 1926 Rose Bowl (which Alabama won 20-19 for their first national championship), Alabama racked up 496 yards of total offense, including 404 on the ground, and seven touchdowns in the shutout. The Tide rolled to 24 first-quarter points to put the game out of reach early en route to an 11-1 season, the Southeast Conference Championship, and a Sugar Bowl victory over Penn State. For James and the Huskies, the loss marked a decisive turning point. James took the blame solely on his shoulders, heeding the advice he had picked up years earlier from Bear Bryant who recommended coaches give credit in victory and take blame in defeat.

When the Huskies returned after their long flight to the Deep South, James had decided to get even closer to his work. That night, he slept on his office couch in the UW Tubby Graves Building. In fact, the first-year head coach grabbed his pajamas and a toothbrush and moved into his office from Sunday to Wednesday of each week—for the remaining six weeks of the season.

James told me that he wanted to send a message to the team that he was completely committed to their success and expected the same dedication from everyone on the team. James said he realized that before any lasting change could begin, he and the Huskies would need to endure some old-fashioned pain and suffering. At the depth of their despair, when he sensed many players simply wanted the season to end and the punishment to stop, James modeled true leadership. He taught the Huskies how to use their suffering to unite and depend upon each other to achieve their goals.

James' actions demonstrated to the Huskies that their new leader was tougher and more determined than most had imagined. Without uttering a word, he moved into his office and modeled for every man on the team his intense resolve to win no matter the cost. He explained to the team how every player—from starters to fourth-stringers—could help the Huskies become relevant again in major college football.

James' commitment would form the bedrock of his legend—sparking the Huskies to fight within a hairsbreadth of the Pacific-8 Conference crown and the Rose Bowl in just his first season.

Reflecting on the 1975 season years later, James said he wanted his players and assistants to understand the depth of his commitment to re-establishing a championship program.

"We had a senior-laden team. When I got here there were very few sophomores and juniors, there were about 40 seniors," he said. "I just kind of had the feeling—we had a new staff and we had just got killed in three of the first five games—that they were kind of hoping it was over, that they were looking forward to getting done with football and getting on with their lives."

Instead of punishing players with a scrimmage on Sunday, the day after the Alabama loss, as many other coaches certainly would have done, James held himself most accountable. For answers to salvage his first Husky season, he looked first in the mirror before focusing his gaze outward.

"One thing a lot of coaches will do when you get beat like we did at Alabama is take you outside and scrimmage. Well they got beat up Saturday, then you beat them up Sunday? In a way, how are you going to get them ready to play? So I felt like a fair message, and I didn't tell anybody, I didn't tell any of the coaches, I just slept on the couch. It saved me a half-hour. It gave me a little more work time. Our locker room shower was right downstairs, so I could shower and shave, everything was right there."

No one associated with the Huskies, aside from James' wife Carol, knew he was moving into Husky football headquarters for the balance of the season. James expected the players would eventually learn of his move into his office—but he didn't want to tell them.

"Someone, a janitor, saw me in my pajamas early one morning, and the word kind of got out," he said. "But it got out to the team that I hadn't given up on the season. And it was an important season, too."

Blaming the players for the loss would have been both wrong and counterproductive, he said.

"Coaches like to take things out on their players. I was going to take some blame and I wasn't going to punish them," he said. "We're going to believe in what we were doing and keep working, but we hadn't given up. I think it helped."

Things would get better soon for the 1975 Huskies and their first-year head coach.

Another Loss Steels James' Resolve
October 23, 1975

One week after the Alabama loss, the Huskies nearly beat Stanford at home on Oct. 18, losing 24-21. If the Huskies had not missed an extra point in that contest, they could have kicked a field goal to win when they were deep in Stanford territory. While playing much better was encouraging for James and the Huskies, the loss brought their record to 2-4, which inspired even more determination from James and the Huskies.

In his Thursday speech on Oct. 23, before the Oregon State game, James' tone turned decidedly indignant. He said the Huskies' record should "disgust" players, and urged them to harness their disgust to whip the underdog Beavers. In an effort to prevent an upset, James offered the Huskies a lesson on the anatomy of upsets.

If a favorite wins, it's expected. If an underdog wins, it's an upset. I'm discussing this today not to be negative but to explore and understand first what makes up an upset and to insure that it does not happen to us. We're a better team, we have earned the right to be the favorite and should be as we're the better team. We don't ever want this "upset" tag on us. Upsets happen each week.

Ingredients of an Upset:

1. One team lacks respect for another, players or coaches.

2. Preparation.

    Coaches:

    - Don't spend the time;
    - Don't dig into film;
    - Don't figure the stats—the percentages;
    - Don't pay attention to detail—look for tips;
    - They make negative comments about opponents, disrespectful;
    - They allow things to slip by—accept less than players' best performances;
    - The result: an inferior plan and poor preparation.

    Players:

    - Players read papers and look at scores.
    - They don't analyze things and just assume the opponent is not strong.
    - They don't spend study time.

Plan and Scout Report:

- Players don't spend the film time;
- They don't get as excited about (medical) treatment—slow to heal;
- They don't spend as much time in mental preparation;
- The result: Inferior physical and mental preparation.

Now, in the meantime, the underdog:

- Has more to gain, not so much to lose.
- Works harder.
- Prepares better.
- Tries harder.
- Has a better plan.
- Gets a better staff effort.
- Is harder-hitting.
- More alert.
- Has greater desire.

These are the ingredients of an upset.

James then reminded the Huskies that their program philosophy aims to develop mature competitors who work hard in practice, regardless of being tired or sore.

Win or lose, they work hard. They work hard regardless of weather. Individual: Never lets anyone beat him in drills—competes. His attitude towards winning never changes. Individual: Extreme distaste for lack of success. Everyone: Going to do something to make things better. Everyone: Work, run, lift, study, recruit.

Thoroughbred people and teams are not upset. They are always competing at their best.

They worked for something and don't want to lose it. Texas, Alabama, Ohio State, Notre Dame, are these kind of teams. They go into 10 or 11 games each year favored. Someone's always trying to knock them off, but seldom do. Why? They have established maturity in their programs. Even if a frosh comes in and plays he's expected to compete, expected to win. Our program philosophy again is designed to treat all opponents equal. Structured approach but not so sophisticated that we cannot adjust or attempt to improve on it. But never overlook any opponent.

What now must we do with our Final 48 Hours? Respect OSU—fear their potential. Be disgusted with our record and committed to improve it. See that there are no flaws in our mental approach and preparation. Believe that we will win and that we will go to the Rose Bowl. Prepare ourselves as a team to dominate OSU on offense, defense and kicking game.

Quarterback Chris Rowland threw a 56-yard touchdown pass to tight end Gordy Bronson early in the third period to break the game open as the Huskies went on to an easy 35-7 win.

From Misdirection, Huskies Find Success

Eager to see how good they could be, the 3-4 Huskies went on a tear—whipping UCLA , Southern California and Washington State. The only defeat in their final five games was a three-point loss at California. The Huskies went from an 0-2 start of the 1975 campaign to finish 6-5—Washington's first winning season since 1972.

It was an incredibly positive finish to a season that would likely have been disastrous had James not committed fully to the turnaround, demonstrated most visibly by moving into the Tubby Graves Building. Slowly and surely, confidence was building in this coach from Kent State, the school immortalized by Neil Young's Vietnam War-era protest song "Ohio." The song was written in reaction to the shootings of May

4, 1970 when the Ohio National Guard opened fire for 13 seconds on student protesters, killing four students and wounding nine. James became Kent State's new head football coach only seven months after the shootings—another challenge that helped form him into the person who would come to define excellence for Washington football.

Nick Saban, head coach at the University of Alabama, was a Kent State freshman at the time of the shootings and told *USA Today* (2010) that he still remembers students lying on the ground, helicopters overhead, and ambulances rushing away. In the fall of 1970, the student body united in an effort to show "that wasn't a reflection of who we were," Saban said. For his part, James sought to make football a force for campus unity. In 1972, James led Kent State to the Mid-American Conference Championship and a trip to the Tangerine Bowl—helping to distance the school from its tragic past.

Just as he had done at Kent State, James had raised hopes and excitement in Husky football once again. By the end of his first season at Washington, the players, alumni, students, and fans knew all about Don James—from his unmatched work ethic to his fierce competitiveness and brilliant game plans. As he had hoped they would, James' players recommitted to the 1975 season after hearing that their leader had moved into his office after the Alabama loss.

James said his move into the office delivered the message he intended the Huskies hear.

What, specifically, was that message?

"That I hadn't given up on that season," James said. "And it was an important season, too."

The Huskies became believers. Just as James suggested, they used the loss at Alabama to turn the season around.

"We beat both L.A. schools and we beat the three Northwest schools," James said. UCLA went to the Rose Bowl, but it could easily have been the Huskies who were Pasadena-bound in James' first season.

"We weren't a Rose Bowl team, but we got them fired up and the guys got excited," James said. If the Huskies had beaten Stanford, they could have kicked a field goal to tie California (instead of going for a touchdown and the win) and would have gone to the Rose Bowl.

"That's how close we were that first year," James said.

More importantly to James and the future of Washington football, the players understood the commitment that would be necessary to reach the Rose Bowl—a goal the Huskies would achieve in James' third season.

Rising from the ashes of an Alabama scorching, James made the Huskies—and the naysayers—believers.

Suddenly, no one was laughing at James' bowl game philosophy.

Suddenly, all eyes were on Washington and their surprising new coach who led the Huskies out of the desert and in clear sight of the Promised Land.

Highly recruited tailback Joe Steele said Coach James told him the Huskies would play in two bowl games if he came to Washington. "And we did. We played in the Rose Bowl when I was a sophomore and then the Sun Bowl in my senior year," Steele said. *UW Photo*

— 1976 —

An Eye-Opener for a Freshman from Spokane

In 1976, James' second year as head coach, the Huskies lost nearly 40 seniors to graduation. Consequently, most observers conceded it would be a year of rebuilding for Washington—although James, as always, planned to win immediately. Warren Moon became Washington's starting quarterback. I reported for my first fall Husky football camp in mid-August as a skinny 18-year-old, 6-foot-1-inch, 190-pound freshman inside linebacker from Gonzaga Prep in Spokane, Washington. The size of my teammates, their strength, speed, and overall athleticism were stunning to me. Needless to say, I had never been a part of a team with so many great athletes. All or most of us freshmen soon became friends—including Vern Olson, a linebacker and my roommate; Joe Steele, the talented tailback from Seattle's Blanchet High School; linebackers Bret Gagliardi and Jimmy Pence; Ron Gipson, a bruising and swift fullback from Everett, Washington; Tom Flick, quarterback; cornerback Mark Lee; defensive tackle Doug Martin and so many others. We bonded through our grueling twice-daily practices in which we would lose 5 pounds or more each practice.

Classes did not begin for several weeks after football practices began, so the coaches had our full attention and demanded our complete commitment, which seemed fair since we all had full-ride scholarships. Husky football became the center of our lives for the next four years. In ways that we had not considered at the time, the experience would shape our lives. Each two-hour practice ran like a Swiss watch—leaving little time to catch our breath. Always, it seemed, we were either exhausting ourselves in one drill or another or running to the next drill. The practices in the stifling August heat, a moister heat and far more humid than I was accustomed to in Spokane, sapped our energies almost completely. We shuffled around Husky football complex, trying our best to reserve as much energy as possible. At training table dinner in the Husky Crew House, it seemed we couldn't drink enough water, juice, lemonade and milk to replace the fluid we lost in those summer practices.

On one of our first evenings at camp, several of us freshmen huddled together in the main-floor meeting room of the Tubby Graves Building, waiting for Coach James to conduct our first team meeting. Always well-fed at training table, we were licking our lips, happily shooting the breeze after devouring thick and delicious T-bone steak, mashed potatoes and gravy, vegetables, and apple or peach pie, or both, piled with vanilla ice cream as high as we liked. It was uncomfortably warm and muggy as James arrived—as always, precisely on time. All chatter in the room instantly fell silent as James walked to the podium and began to describe for us the tough two weeks ahead in which we would experience "the Spartan life." James suggested we accept two-a-days as a highly structured, grueling period in our lives in which we would experience the virtues of hard work, sacrifice and discipline. While we knew it would not be easy, few of us, it seemed, realized how demanding the training camp would be.

James told the team that our toughness and commitment to become champions would be tested, that our bodies would be battered and sore, but that it was all necessary to prepare ourselves mentally and physically to accomplish our mission: win the conference championship, advance to the Rose Bowl, and win it. Our tolerance for pain and suffering, he said, would be stretched beyond what we had ever experienced. He predicted, correctly, that some players would quit—unwilling or unable to pay the "awful price" to become champions. Those of us who endured, James promised, would be a part of something great and lasting—something most people could only dream of experiencing. Those of us who were tough enough to last, he said, would know we went through something most people could never endure.

Those of us unwilling to pay the price were neither welcome nor worthy to call themselves Huskies, he said. We had a chance to achieve something together, as a team, James said, that would be far greater than anything most of us might achieve on our own. We had a chance, he said, to achieve something that would live far beyond our flashes of youthful athleticism. Being very clear, he said this opportunity would exact a tremendous toll. However, if we committed to pay the price of success, James said our dreams to capture the Pac-8 crown, play in the Rose Bowl, and win it would come true.

Becoming Rose Bowl champions, he said, would become a tremendous family treasure for each of us to pass on to our children—an achievement that we would carry with us for the rest of our lives.

I believed Don James' promises—I think most of us did.

In an interview with Coach James long after my playing days had ended, he told me that his "Spartan Life" message helped set the tone and tenor for each season—especially for the freshmen and transfers.

"It was just that what we're going to do these two or three weeks is not going to be a lot of fun, but it's going to make us tougher," James said. "If you set that before them, 'Well, I know this is going to be tough, but I'm going to take pride in the fact that we went through this together with these guys. We're going to get better because of it. It's important, we need it, and it's going to help us.' If you can go in with that attitude that 'nothing is too tough for me, I can handle it' then you can get through it and the camaraderie develops—a feeling that we went through something that very few people in this country could ever go through."

Certainly, the work we endured together unified our team of individuals toward our common purpose.

A Sense of Certain Success

As a freshman, I noticed many of the veterans on our team seemed to exude a quiet confidence. Not smugness or conceit, it was more an air of confident expectation. I felt an almost tangible sense that we were destined for the Rose Bowl. Later in my freshman year, during spring practices, I came to feel almost certain that our team—full of lively characters and packed with talent—was ready for a break-out season. At home for Christmas as a freshman, I told my parents I would not be coming home for Christmas the next year, "because we are going to the Rose Bowl." As it turned out, many of my teammates shared the feeling.

The Huskies maintained dominion over the three other Northwest schools in the 1976 season and beat Minnesota and Virginia while losing to Colorado, Indiana, Stanford, UCLA, California, and USC—finishing 5-6, James' one losing season at UW. Nevertheless, many of James' most important and inspiring themes, those he would refer to in his Thursday speeches throughout his UW career, emerged in this his second season leading the Huskies.

Those speeches follow.

'Whatever It Takes—We Must Do'
September 23, 1976

We started the 1976 campaign with a decisive 38-17 win at home over Virginia before losing the following week to Colorado 21-7, also in Husky Stadium. In this, his Thursday speech prior to hosting Indiana, James asked us to consider how our loss to Colorado might benefit us. There would be no gain from the loss, he said, without pain. In another discussion of competitive greatness, a prominent theme of the Thursday speeches, James said he was focused solely on winning and that we had better be as well.

> We're no longer discussing our youth or inexperience. We're beyond that. I've decided, no more excuses for us. Be absolute. No bullshit. Do it! I've mentioned "to hell with doing our best.

To hell with giving 100 percent." Our motto now is, "Whatever it takes—we must do! You—me—everyone in here!"

We've got to understand the winning EDGE. Our program design has it. We simply take the word "EDGE" and turn it into an acronym, giving each letter additional meaning:

E—Extra study. We must be able to carry out the details of our assignments in a stress situation on Saturday. We work on this five weeks during fall camp. We work on it in meetings, film sessions, tests, Friday review. I don't know of any team in the country that does more to prepare or cut mental errors. Men, great physical talent is useless if we don't cut mental errors. Master your plan through review mentally.

D—Determination. Set your mind to what you want to do and do whatever it takes to get it (within the rules). There are many examples of great determination on this squad—let's get even more.

G—Great Conditioning. Gassers, progressives for more stamina and more endurance to outscore opponents in the second half.

E—Extra Effort. Bust your ass; fight for that extra yard. You must now be programming yourself for the game. We make you do it right in practice. The winning edge comes in three broad areas: mental (extra study), physical (practice field and weights) and emotional (determination). This requires total involvement.

Emotional involvement means everything. I never want to say after a ball game:

"Our opponents wanted the game more than we did."

"Our opponents were more ready to play than we were."

"They were more determined to play than we were or their emotions were higher."

I will have to admit that some teams may be more physical but never, ever should an opponent want a game more than we.

We all realize that our opponents have plays—and that they play defense. They practice. They want respect. This winning EDGE, then, becomes the standard for any players that want to perform on this Husky team.

You must not only understand the EDGE concept, you must be willing and ready to make the sacrifices necessary to make the standard and produce the end result: to gain an EDGE over the opponent. The challenge then is to establish a standard of excellence for now and in the future. Our theme for this week: work for perfection.

The last item. When we face adversity, something goes wrong. I've said (Monday) the value received from defeat will be in direct proportion to our suffering. Great competitors make others pay. There were two or three examples last Saturday. Alabama 56-3, SMU paid. USC 53-0, Oregon paid. Nebraska 45-13, Indiana paid. Well it's time now that the Huskies make someone pay. We didn't schedule the game. They're next! We have got to take a determined, cold, clinical approach to this one. We have the EDGE. With our hitting and flying around, let's build on it.

Indiana snapped a 10-game losing streak to beat us 20-13, bringing our record to 1-2. While showing glimpses of improvement, this Husky team had a long way to go to realize its potential. The team recovered quickly to beat Minnesota 38-7 in Husky Stadium the following week to bring our record even at 2-2 before our first Pac-8 Conference game at Oregon State the following Saturday, Oct. 9.

James Introduces 'Possibility Thinking'
October 7, 1976

In his Thursday speech before the Oregon State game, James urged each player to use the bus ride to Corvallis wisely by concentrating on his role in the game. He called the Oregon State game "Step No. 1 to the Championship" and delivered a stirring talk about "possibility thinking," a term that emerges in his Thursday speeches several times during his early years at Washington.

It's Possible!

Is it possible for an overweight 59-year-old man, who has never been an athlete, who looks and feels older than his age, is it possible for such a man to become a record-breaking long distance runner? It's possible. It happened—he even qualified for the Boston Marathon.

Can a cerebral-palsied quadriplegic learn to walk? It's possible.

Can a near high school dropout become one of the world's leading brain surgeons? It's possible.

Is it possible for a poor athlete who was told he was too dumb for college and that he should take shop in high school and learn a trade. Is it possible for this man to attain a college diploma, become a pro star, and receive a law degree? It's possible! It happened!

Many people, especially those who think negatively, would say that all of these things are impossible. But these people believed and made the changes to see their goals accomplished.

Think of this: She's barely 20 years old. She speaks only Spanish when she arrives in Los Angeles with $7 in her pocket. She saves $400, starts a taco business, turns it into a multimillion-dollar operation and becomes treasurer of the United States of America. Is this possible? Well, it happened! She is Romana Banuelos.

Is it possible for the Washington Huskies to dare to dream of a championship? We were picked to finish last!

We were all openly and secretly dissatisfied with our level of success—with our status one week ago. We want to be able to really be proud of ourselves and still not lose genuine humility.

Then keep dreaming! It's Possible! You can become the team you've always wanted to be!

How? There is a key. There is a secret. There is a way—to turn impossible dreams into fantastic accomplishments.

It's called Possibility Thinking. Some call it faith. Here's how it works! When you, we begin to believe it might be possible—some how, some way, some day—three miracles occur.

The First Miracle

- Opportunity-spotting brain cells activate.
- You run a little harder, and say to yourself, 'I can get open.'
- You run a little faster, 'I can get my man.'
- You get to the ball and recover a fumble.

The Second Miracle

- Problem-solving brain cells come to life, solving every problem and making us stronger.
- We say, 'I'll find a way.'
- If we're not taxed and we don't have to think and re-act, we don't stay alert and cautious—we're lulled to sleep. We can't pick up blitzes and can't adjust to new plays.

Third Miracle

- Determination-energizing chemicals are released into the bloodstream!
- If you were not determined you wouldn't be here.
- If you were not determined, you wouldn't have taken apart Minnesota!
- With possibility thinking, we must become more de-termined.
- Persistence—stay with it.

- Patience to not expect it's easy right now. We must endure.

Your staff played this game. It took approximately 150 man-hours. It's the Possibility Thinking Game. Coaches all over the Northwest have heard about this and requested copies!

Rules:

1. Agree to listen

2. Agree to care

3. Ask tough questions

4. Innovate

5. Assume success

Objective: Win Rose Bowl January 1, 1977

- What will it take?

- 10 Major Areas:

- Strength—Plans—Eligibility—Offense—Defense—etc.

- Our program philosophy is the result (of the Possibility Thinking Game).

Think of This:

- In front of you is an invisible staircase.

- It rises higher and higher, basically it has 8 steps.

- Conference championship: 7 stairs.

- Win Rose Bowl: 8 stairs.

- Feel yourself rise.

- You will become the team you want to be!

- The higher you climb—the farther you'll see!

- Self-confidence will begin to surge within you. In fact you can begin to feel it from last week's game. I can see it in you!

- Unbelievable surprises await you at the top of the staircase. Start today!
- <u>Some people suffer hell because they lack the faith to believe and begin.</u>
- So many people have proven this.

To recap, when we begin to believe three miracles occur:

1. Opportunity-spotting cells activate.

2. Problem-solving cells come to life.

3. Determination-energizing chemicals are released.

Next 46 hours think! Dream!

It's possible with a footnote: It's one step at a time.

Start by kicking the hell out of O.S.U.

Freshman tailback Joe Steele, who took over after starter Ron Rowland injured an ankle, scored touchdowns on runs of one and three yards to lead the Huskies to a 24-12 win over the Beavers as we improved our record to 3-2.

Tale of the Tiger Cage
October 14, 1976

James began his Thursday speech the following week, before we played at Stanford, with an expansion of his possibility thinking theme. He also offered the memorable story of the "Tiger Cage Principle."

It's Possible

Predictions. Washington was predicted to finish last. We've already passed one team on the staircase. Look where they picked our opponent this week, second.

Review: Three miracles that occur.

1. Opportunity. Alert defense destroyed OSU, got turn-overs and what great opportunities.

2. Problem Solving. Penalty, two fumbles left us with more problems but second quarter we solved and executed with perfection—we were lacking here in the second half.

3. Determination chemicals. OSU athletes were also determined and in some cases more so.

Stanford players were very determined against UCLA. This is a characteristic of the level of competition that we are at.

It will not work if we don't:

1) Work at it.

2) Concentrate on it!

3) Cover every detail and every potential eventuality.

So I ask, how can we let Stanford be more determined than us?

Of all the persons living on earth, there is only one person who has the power to cast the deciding vote to kill your dream. That person is you. You cast the death sentence to your dream when you decide to quit dreaming, stop trying, and give up.

James said that we, the 1976 Huskies, could be considered "caged," but could free ourselves to achieve our potential if we let go of our preconceived definitions of success, and practiced possibility thinking. Those who refused to be positive were "impossibility thinkers," James told us, before sharing the following story, which he said illustrates how negative thoughts might be preventing the team from reaching its potential.

The Tiger Cage Principle

Definition: What is a tiger cage? Basically it is a relatively small cage made of bamboo sticks for capturing tigers. During the Vietnam War the Viet Cong, communist guerrillas in South Vietnam, were constantly on the move through the jungles.

They kept their POWs (Prisoners of War) not in fixed camps but in small portable prisons that could be picked up and moved.

Year after year, men were living in a cage 5-feet long, 4-feet high. Many men spent as many as four years in these cages, one spent six years. One night a Navy flier succeeded in working one bamboo stick loose. "That was all I needed to step out and I was free," he said.

So his objective was to get free. All the bamboo poles helped keep him a prisoner. But it took only one to set him free. Teams sometimes get trapped in a Tiger Cage with many things representing bars and it really only takes the removal of one to insure being successful.

Bars represent for us: fear of failure. Headlines paralyze impossibility thinkers. Problems mobilize possibility thinkers: interceptions, missed blocks, many missed tackles, blocked kicks. Many times if a team will just remove one of these items, it can set itself free.

People say, "I can't. I'm at the end of my rope." I say, "Hell, tie a knot and hang on." This is how we escape from the Tiger Cage: Remember your objective, practice Possibility Thinking, and figure out a way to get it done.

You now need to focus on taking care of your own individual area: All blockers—block like hell. Tackle up and through, and knock the ball out. Ball carriers—never fumble. Pass receivers—catch it or get it down, don't tip to defense. Penalties—don't line up onside, if official blows us for it that's one setback we can't afford it. Problems—figure out a way.

James closed this Thursday speech with yet another story about positive thinking. If we don't try for the "big fish," a truly worthy purpose, or if we do not expect to "catch" it, he said, we will not be prepared to seize such opportunities when they occur.

Good Things Happen to Big-Thinking People

A tourist walked down a pier and watched a fisherman pull in a large fish, measure it, and throw it back. He caught a second fish, smaller this time, he measured it, and put it in his basket. Oddly, all fish over 10 inches, he discarded. The smaller ones, he kept.

Someone asked him, "why?" The fisherman said, "Because my frying pan only measures 10 inches." Is that foolish? Of course it is, but it's no more so than when we throw away the biggest ideas and most beautiful dreams that come into your mind simply because your experience is too limited. Start growing now. Start thinking. Big things happen to big-thinking people. You can become the team you want to be. It's possible. Every man must make his contribution.

Quarterback Warren Moon rallied the six-point underdog Huskies to a pair of touchdowns in the final six minutes but it wasn't enough as Stanford won 34-28, bringing our record to 3-3.

On Freud, Frankl, and Faith
November 4, 1976

After narrowly beating Oregon 14-7 in Husky Stadium, we lost to UCLA 30-21 the following week, also at home, bringing our record to 4-4. While competitive, often against much more experienced teams, trouble lurked below the surface of this team. The problems among players included flaring tempers and finger pointing. No one, neither the coaches nor the players, was satisfied with the progress of the program in James' second season. In his Thursday speech before we hosted California, James addressed the problems. Expecting the full heat of a fiery Don James, he surprised us all by opening with a Bible verse about love—the last thing any of us expected in a pre-game speech.

We all want to be a part of a successful team organization. Everyone plays a part with our growth or deterioration. What part will you play? A problem or a solution to problems! From John 1, Chapter 3, Verse 18 (the first letter of John). "Let us not love in word or speech, but in deed and in truth." We can say things, but it's more important to do and to show this attitude. As I have mentioned, the team doesn't stay the same—it's either up or down.

With respect to the high goals the Huskies set for the season, James introduced the ideas of Sigmund Freud and Viktor Frankl, two enormously influential psychological thinkers of the modern age, who came to espouse radically different theories. In this speech, James offers a glimpse of his scholarly prowess as he points out their different approaches to goal setting. James favors Frankl's positive-thinking view.

The fear of failure deteriorates preparation confidence. Now, wipe out the fear of failure and move ahead to become the team we want to be. To succeed, we must eliminate once and for all the persistent problem called fear of failure. We can dream up ideas—creative ideas. But until we wipe out fear of failure our projects will have difficulty getting off the ground. This may explain why negative-thinking Sigmund Freud objected to goal setting. He saw the potential dangers. Unfulfilled goals generate illness-producing anxiety and frustration, he contended. It also explains why another Viennese psychiatrist, positive-thinking Viktor Frankl, insists on goal setting. He sees possibilities. A lack of goals removes all meaning from being, he states.

The truth is both Freud and Frankl are right! The solution, however, is not to fear goals, but to wipe out fear of failure. We do this by redefining the meaning of failure. Some thoughts on this: Failure doesn't mean we are a failure; it does mean we haven't succeeded yet. Failure doesn't mean we have accomplished nothing; it does mean we have learned something. Failure doesn't mean we've been disgraced; it does mean we were willing to try.

No force, no emotion is more paralyzing than fear. It stops people from making moves that they must make to succeed. (There have been risks, gambles taken in every season's story; take a chance, gamble.) In the whole sorry spectacle of human fears none is more destructive and defeating than fear of failure. Eject this fear out of your life.

Faith. If you don't try because you are afraid that you may have to work harder, sacrifice more or get involved, that is dishonorable. When you try again and again and demonstrate dedication, courage, faith and self-sacrifice you will attract a whole new set of real friends, those who give your self-respect a boost.

James then shared the well-documented story of 154 people, judged by society to be "hopelessly insane," who escaped from a mental hospital. Later, more than half of these former mental patients were found living perfectly normal lives.

Hopelessly Insane?

Richard Lemon, in an article titled "The Uncertain Science" (in *The Saturday Evening Post*, Aug. 10, 1968), tells about an occurrence at a mental hospital in a Paris suburb during the Second World War. The institution housed 154 cases that were judged by the best psychiatrists to be hopelessly insane. One dark night the invading armies of liberation shelled the walls off the hospital. In the ensuing confusion, all 154 escaped. Many years later when they finally tracked down each of those patients, they were amazed to find that 86 out of 154 had completely recovered and were living perfectly normal and productive lives.

So you have to ask, at this point, "What, then, is a real failure?" The answer becomes clear: Real failure is to fail as a person, to yield to cowardice in the face of a difficult task. We have three difficult tasks coming up. How will faith help us? Bust your butt because you know that every man is busting his—not 49 of 50 like we had last week. Running backs, when the ball comes, blow up in there because you have faith in your line.

Pass defenders, play a slow catch type coverage when a pass rush is called because you have faith that pressure will be applied on the quarterback. And you can go on and on and turn each of these analogies around. Linemen busting their butts to make a hole because they know that a running back is coming hell-bent for election and is expecting a hole to be there.

We get this right and we are on our way: Eliminate fear of failure; have faith in each other.

We lost to California 7-0. Sophomore quarterback Duane Akina replaced starter Warren Moon in the third quarter after Moon was shaken up.

Competitive Greatness
November 11, 1976

In his Thursday speech before we traveled to Los Angeles to play heavily favored USC, James revisited the topic of competitive greatness. The 7-1 Trojans, led by Coach John Robinson, were loaded with talent, including consensus All-Americans Ricky Bell at running back (plus backs Charles White and Mosi Tatupu), offensive tackle Marvin Powell, and defensive back Dennis Thurman. In James' second UW season, we were fighting to improve our 4-5 record.

> Competitive Greatness. Average people produce under pressure generated by events, circumstances of other people who control their lives. Exceptional persons produce under urgent pressure they have deliberately generated themselves! In other words, for mature competitors, pressure is self-imposed. We must determine for ourselves, each one of us, how we are to apply pressure on ourselves—get ourselves motivated to have competitive greatness this Saturday.
>
> This is our theme for this week: COMPETITIVE GREATNESS. Each individual fitting his small piece into the

puzzle of a game plan. We must figure out a way to successfully complete your job. Don't wait; slow movers are low-
achievers. Opportunities don't wait for slow-thinking people.
Many times upsets come because the underdog gets into a
game and—because of a set of circumstances—they learn that
they can really compete with this team. They start to say, "Hey
guys! We can whip them. They're not what they have been
built up to be! They're not superhuman." There would be
many more upsets if more teams would go into a game confident that they can compete and win.

One writer asked me today if our team is going in with the
idea that we would be satisfied if we can just make it close—
keep the score down—make USC struggle to win. I told him
"Hell No! There was no place in our program for that kind of
thinking." I told him, "Our sights are set on becoming the best
and in order to become the best you have to beat the best."

James reminded the Huskies that USC had had two close games that
season: Missouri and Purdue.

Missouri whipped them! Because they are tougher than hell.
They didn't back down. They knocked hell out of the Trojans.
They fought like hell. Got their licks in. Missouri won (46-25).
Purdue couldn't stop (plays) 24 & 25; the fullback killed them.
But they were sure in the battle and I'm sure they beat Michi-
gan because of this fighting attitude.

James then exhorted us to "snap the cords of laziness, break the chains
of lethargy"—saying "winning starts with beginning! Wake up! Come
alive!"

"Remember," he said, "slow-movers are low-achievers."

Make up your mind to act *now*! Do it *now*! Take some action
now! Do it this afternoon on the practice field carry it through
preparations until kickoff. Then be absolute! Do it during the
game. Shake up the negative thoughts. Shake all impossibility

thoughts out of your mind. Shake them out! Be strong. Be confident! Break up the obstacles. Shatter those barriers.

James reminded us of his words earlier that season about how great teams expect adversity and respond positively.

> We all expected adversity—we talked about it in early fall. We respond by getting stronger and more determined. The way to make a doorway in the Great Wall of China is by removing one rock at a time. Football is the game! Fight for 60 minutes, one play at a time, fight for every precious yard. Then you'll walk away with the honors. People will respect and admire you. You'll become the person you always wanted to be. You'll become the team you wanted to become. Your biggest obstacle is getting started—you can eliminate that! Right Now!

> Competitive Greatness—it's our weekly theme! Many in here would like to advance into the NFL, pro ball. What better way to be evaluated than blocking, tackling, competing against great players? Most pro scouts feel USC has at least five first-round draft picks, five! You want to enhance your position? Whip those five! Scouts always want to compare you in great competition, not how you do versus poor players. Our Monday Theme was "be at your best when your best is needed." This is the best team on our schedule—the most physical team and the most talented. We surely need each man's best!

> Our Tuesday Theme: A real love of hard battle! These are the games remembered for a lifetime! People won't talk about beating Virginia or Oregon in 1976. They will talk for years about the great wins. Purdue beat Michigan—they immediately referred to 1950 when Purdue beat Notre Dame 26 years ago—great win (the Boilermakers snapped Notre Dame's 39-game unbeaten string). Do you know who beat Purdue the next week? University of Miami and there were 100,000 people at the airport. You'll talk about the plays and the battle wounds inflicted on them and us for years.

Our Wednesday Theme: When the Going Gets Tough, the Tough Get Going! How old, yet how true! We see some fantastic individual feats in games like this one. There is a need for 54 tough SOBs to get on that plane in the morning.

Our Thursday Theme: End the Conquest. I think you are as tired as I am of seeing that Coliseum scoreboard light up after each SC score. "The Conquest goes on." Everyone in Los Angeles is thinking and talking about next week when UCLA plays USC. Wow! What a game. A sellout! Great rivalry! Both L.A. schools playing for the championship—conference and national—and the bowls. Every writer, TV, radio station is looking at our game as some sort of a second-class preliminary contest. "Scrimmage: UCLA vs. OSU, USC vs. UW." They ask, "What do you think of two schools? Rate them! Who will win? How does it feel to be a preliminary?" They don't ask about us, about our guys. They have the nerve to call and ask about UCLA and USC. That's what we mean by "End the Conquest." Let's let the big prelim be the final bout, the Main Attraction. Let's screw up their big TV date. Let's make them pay a big price for overlooking us. Let's get after their ass!

Vince Evans threw a 24-yard scoring strike and connected on a 46-yard pass to set up a second touchdown to lead USC to a 20-3 victory at the Coliseum. The following week, we beat WSU 51-32 to close out the 1976 season. Swirling beneath the surface were growing expectations for the program from fans and the media. However, the greatest expectations were being generated by James and the Huskies.

Buoyed by rising talent and motivated with the spirit of unlimited possibilities and a chip-on-the-shoulder attitude, we were beginning to appreciate the meaning of competitive greatness as James had explained it. No one was more anxious for the 1977 season to begin than Washington's coaches and players. We knew our hard work and James' inspired leadership had formed the foundation for something special.

Doug Martin was an imposing figure at defensive tackle for the Huskies and one of James' prize recruits in the early years of his program.

UW Photo

— 1 9 7 7 —

The Season Begins: A Focus on Mental Preparation
September 8, 1977

We launched the 1977 season at home on Sept. 10 against the tough and talented Bulldogs of Mississippi State, ranked No. 16 in the country. James opened his Thursday speech with a focus on mental preparation—another major theme of his speeches.

> Final sharpening of our team effort comes in two ways: Rest and elaborate on the game. Mental focus. The weights, sprints, and contact are now over. Today's drills are primarily review. So why worry about it? What's so important about mental preparation? We're not like any other sport. We don't play 80 to 150 games a season. We play 11 and hopefully 12 (bowl game) and must perform at a very high level, high standard. You need quiet time to lock in quietly on the job. It's proven—performance levels rise.

> You've all proven it during your career. To take a test, you study and prepare to do well. Transcendental meditation. The idea is to block out distractions and lock in our your job. What can we expect to get out of these next 44 and one-half hours by focusing mentally?

> • Master your plan totally—whether it's offense, defense, or kicking game.

> • You become stronger.

- You become tougher.
- You play above your ability—or reach your potential.
- You have a pre-play edge and have access to mental tips of your opponent's tendencies.
- It slows down the game for you.
- You can free-flow in the game.
- Makes for more alert team play.

James then explained the proud and rich football heritage of Mississippi State in the powerful Southeast Conference where college football is arguably as important as religion. In a 2012 article in *ESPN The Magazine,* Rick Bragg captured the culture of college football in the South with a story about a rare Alabama loss in the Bear Bryant era.

As the story goes, Bryant's sidekick on his weekly TV show said: "The Lord just wasn't with us, Coach."

"The Lord," Bryant said, "expects you to block and tackle."

James reminded us that the SEC is the home of Alabama, which destroyed Washington in James' first UW season.

> You remember Alabama. The SEC takes pride in having an average of four to five teams each year in bowls. They have pride in their quickness, toughness. We must respect them but not hold them in awe. I think we are OK here. Last fall, they (Mississippi State) had an outstanding team—better than ours. Now we're better, we have got to be. They are a nationally ranked team—only one of our first four great challenges. This is a great opportunity. The teams seem pretty even to me. Who will win? The team that handles the ball the best. The team with the most hitters—we've got to get after them! We've got to hit them early and keep on hitting for 60 minutes.

Bruce Threadgill passed for touchdowns of 44 and 81 yards while fullback Dennis Johnson rushed for 113 yards and caught a TD pass to lead MSU to a 27-18 victory. Steve Robbins tied Don Martin's (1966)

UW school record of four field goals in a game with a pair from 31 yards and two more from 28 and 35 yards. Joe Steele returned the opening kickoff 73 yards to the MSU 21 to set up Robbins' first field goal. This was no way to start a championship season and Coach James made sure we knew it.

*Mississippi State and UCLA would forfeit all 11 games in 1977 due to NCAA penalties. As a result, Washington's final (historical) record for 1977 was 10-2, instead of 8-4 (including the Rose Bowl victory over Michigan).

'I Feel This Great Urge, I Feel This Great Need to Compete!'
September 15, 1977

In his Thursday speech the week after the Mississippi State loss, as we prepared to host San Jose State, James had competitive greatness on his mind. Those of us who were on the 1976 team had heard variations on this theme twice in James' Thursday speeches the previous year. As he had told us after the loss to Colorado in 1976, James repeated "someone has to pay." This week, he said, we must make San Jose State pay for our loss to Mississippi State.

> We were defeated by a good team last Saturday. We wanted to win. We prepared to win. We actually tried hard to win—but failed. It was a temporary setback. Respect in college football is an incredible thing. Win last Saturday and we're probably in the Top 20. People respect Mississippi State and the Southeast Conference now. We've got little respect nationally—this could change. We've got San Jose State, then Syracuse, Minnesota and Oregon. We are, therefore, now expected to go into the Stanford game 4-1. Do it and we get no extra respect. Don't do it! People will look down on us and treat us horribly—poor respect.

We had better build proper respect for San Jose State, James cautioned.

If we don't have competitive respect for SJSU, we're in deep trouble. Average people produce under pressure generated by events or other people. Exceptional persons produce under urgent pressures they have deliberately generated themselves. I feel this great urge. I feel this great need to compete! This urge to show people that we are winners—somebody, a team to be reckoned with. In other words, that we are mature competitors. We will impose pressure on ourselves and get ourselves ready for competitive greatness.

We have suffered enough from losing to Mississippi State, James said, adding that it's time to make San Jose State suffer.

Maybe we will not gain respect in our league until we knock off a California school. But we can have a lot fun along the way kicking the crap out of our opponent. One at a time, let's make them all pay.

James then used an affirmation from a Thursday speech in his first season before the Navy game:

Isn't it wonderful what can be accomplished when no one cares who gets the credit. Many teams have this problem—stat-seekers. Got to get the ink—headline-wanters. I've never been around a more unselfish team. I'm totally sold that you people have placed team success over individual glory. My concern is now over outside pressures.

Next, James referenced the booing that senior quarterback Warren Moon endured in Husky Stadium against Mississippi State and said the boos would subside when all the Huskies did their jobs.

Concerning our quarterback, we can all contribute to getting people, fans off our QB's butt. You see, he is being blamed for losing—not the offensive line, not the running backs, receivers or the defense. The quarterback is being blamed. All I'm suggesting is that if we can all go out and play to our potential, we will all win and one player will not have to take the abuse—

booing, etc. for defeat. I expect to take the abuse. I will always get way too much credit and blame—but that's my job. I hesitate to bring this up but felt it was something that we can do internally.

We are picked as favorites, should be. We are a better team but have not proven it yet. They have size enough to play. They have speed—great speed in some areas. They can throw the ball. Everyone knows that passing teams, when clicking, when given the time, can negate physical strength. Improvement area: third down; let's make third downs a crusade—we must convert. Defensive rush—cover react, draw screen. We can't go out and make a team out of them. Remember, the longer we keep the underdog in the game, the tougher he gets.

Joe Steele scored two touchdowns, a 63-yard romp on the fifth play of the game and an 8-yard pass from Warren Moon late in the second period, to lead a 24-3 win over outmatched San Jose State. Steve Robbins' 28-yard field goal made him the most prolific point-scoring kicker in Husky history (at the time) with 152 points. The celebration would be short-lived, however. After losing two consecutive road games by two points each—at Syracuse 22-20 and at Minnesota 19-17—our dreams for the 1977 season seemed to be slipping through our fingers like too much Seattle rain.

'Thick Skin' and 'Get It Going'
October 6, 1977

James' Pyramid of Objectives goals structure was a vital part of the Washington program. However, at this moment in the 1977 season—when we were 1-3, having suffered back-to-back losses—James recognized the need for a different approach. Tossing his personal goal sheet aside, he took action to redirect the Huskies toward our Rose Bowl destiny. Just as the 1975 loss to Alabama catalyzed James and the Huskies to draw within a whisker of reaching the Rose Bowl in his first season, James decided to act off-script to correct our course. After all, he was in the third season of a four-year contract and his overall record was 12-14.

Realizing he could be fired if we played seven more games like our first four, James tore up his goal sheet and wrote two messages on a card: "Thick Skin" and "Get It Going." The messages cued James to stop worrying about what was being said and written about the Huskies, and focused his attention on solutions. As part of this effort, James asked each of us to rewrite our personal goals, which we had drafted at the beginning of the season. This time, he asked us to direct our goals toward this question: "What can I do to help the team *today*?"

On the bright side, although 1-3, we had not yet played a conference game and still controlled our Rose Bowl destiny. A win at Oregon on Saturday would get our team back on track.

James was animated in his Thursday speech before the Oregon game, saying it was time to do or die—to play like we all knew we could but hadn't to date. The sense of urgency in his voice was unmistakable.

> This Is Our Rose Bowl Right Here and Now! We Must Perform NOW! Oregon. First Championship Game? We can label it anything we want. New season—first championship game. I'll tell you what it is—a must game. We must play a solid complementing game. Kicking—offense—defense. Helping each other, not hurting each other. We must win!!

James called this "a worry game" because we were favorites in a rivalry series.

> It's a series that has been won more by UW of late than Oregon—20 of the last 28, eight of the last 12. Huskies have enjoyed more football success the past few years than Oregon. It then tends to become a bigger game to the underdog. This gives them a psychological edge, but it should not. Oregon is fighting for their mere existence, not making enough money to pay for football. These are the reasons this is a worry game—coaches, fans become more concerned about us.

He told us this before recounting his first Oregon game at UW in 1975.

I heard a lot of questions then from our support people who are visible and from alumni, etc. Some of those questions: "Are the guys up?" "Are the guys ready?" "Do they remember 1973 58-0 down there?" "Do they know the spread—victory or defeat (6) of last (8) games?" "Do they know—do they realize that Oregon plays their best vs. UW?" My answer to these questions: "Yes, we realize these things. Yes, we are preparing ourselves." With this in mind, the game's outcome will reflect our performance; how we play determines whether we win. Now we sit here and surely all want to win. Are we prepared to play to win? This is a good test game—a test of our character as a team.

Do we have a championship team? Do we want to perform like champions? With key injuries, will others pick up the slack? Our schedule is a natural for league play. Oregon is easily good enough to win this week. But each week, for the next six games, the teams will increase in degree of difficulty: Oregon, Stanford, Oregon State, UCLA, California, USC. Now ask yourselves these questions:

- Why not play better than you are?

- Why not hit harder than you ever have?

- Why not try harder than you ever have?

- Why not wipe everything from our minds but football for two days?

- Why not eliminate every mental mistake?

Think about how you would play in the seventh game if you have just won six and this one is for the Rose Bowl. Think about how you would perform in the Rose Bowl. Hell men, this is our Rose Bowl right here and now. We must perform now! If we don't have the team character to go and just kick hell out of Oregon, where do you think it's going to come from when you play USC, Ohio State or Michigan? We've set goals, objectives, but hell we haven't scratched the surface of our potential. Football is, or was supposed to be, important. Let's act like it. Let's play like it.

Then, James shared the tale of Vince Papale—a story that would inspire the 2006 movie *Invincible* starring Mark Wahlberg.

How many read *Sports Illustrated* last week? How many know about Vince Papale? There's a man that had a dream—goal. He wanted to play football, just play football. As a senior in high school he finally grew to 5-foot-5 inches, 145 pounds, so he went out and played one year.

He started high school at 4-foot-5-inches and 85 pounds. He got a track scholarship and got a degree from St. Joseph's College in Philadelphia. They don't have football but he still wanted to play. He grew up to be 6-foot-2, 185 pounds. After college graduation, he also wanted to go to the 1972 Olympics in the decathlon. He began working. He had hoped to get enough points to qualify for the Olympic Trials.

As he said "the track establishment treats you like a leper" if you're not in the mainstream. He mailed in an application for the Drake Relays. The director mailed back, "We don't let jerks walk in off the street." His thought, "I'm going to show you who I am you SOB." He framed the letter.

Men, I feel just like that with our detractors now.

Well, he began playing in the Delco League called "rough touch," no pads, hard-hitting, seven men on a side for four years, 1969–72. He had broken ribs, a dislocated jaw. From there, he played for the Aston Knights in 1973, at age 27, a local semipro team. He had 60 receptions, led the league. In 1974 the World Football League came on the scene. Phila-Bell had 800 aspirants. Now 28 years old, he made it. In 1975, the Phila-Bell team went under with the rest. He had written Mike McCormack with the Eagles, and was told "no." When Dick Vermeil took over last fall, Papale finally got his chance.

At rookie camp, he was 30 years old. Then he got invited to fall camp. Survived cuts. He tells about how he trained weights— sprints. This was his last chance. He had this dream. He had to prove himself. He made the team—this year again. Why did he make it? Dick Vermeil said, "He's a character player—we need more like him—not less!" Another coach said, "I've never seen a man play with such intensity. Vince will get knocked down three times, bounce up and still make the tackle. On punts, teams will put three or four blockers against him and even then they can't contain him."

A conservative dreamer?

"Not really," James says, quoting the article. "When you consider that Vince Papale has realized the dream of every aging would-be jock from Hemingway's Robert Cohn through Thurber's Walter Mitty to Sylvester Stallone's Rocky Balboa, then he got to be the most radical dreamer of them all. And he's not fiction."

Well, we should be radical dreamers, then make our dreams come true. Get yourself ready to perform no matter the weather, injuries, whatever. Football is important to this university. It's important to people in this room. Let's play like we can play and Oregon has no chance to be champion. We have the opportunity to become champions. Let's act like it and play like it. If it's important to Vince Papale, it ought to be important to us.

All of James' course-correction strategies worked. The story he told about Vince Papale worked. James' temporary mantras "Thick Skin" and "Get It Going" worked. With a breathtaking show of power, speed, and hitting, the Huskies destroyed Oregon 54-0. As James said later, the Huskies' score could easily have been 70 points. Just as the season seemed to be slipping away, our dream to advance to the 1978 Rose Bowl was back on track, barreling forcefully ahead.

Let's Turn the Stanford Game into a 'Classic...'
October 13, 1977

In his Thursday speech the following week, before we played Stanford, James said the Huskies were physically stronger and better than the two previous Husky teams that lost close games to Stanford (34-28 in 1976 and 24-21 in 1975).

> Two years ago, we blocked two punts, got in close and could have won. We have closed the gap. Stanford as a team, let's examine them. They have a dangerous offense—averaging 439 yards a game, No. 2 in the league. Averaging 266 yards a game passing, No. 1 in the league. Benjamin No. 1 in league. Lofton—best receiver Walsh has coached. Nelson 102 average per game rushing. Nelson 861 yards total offense, 9th in the nation. Offense has what Walsh predicts as three first-round picks Benjamin—Lofton—King. Top 12 picks by pro scouts. Offense has tough kids but basically it's a trick 'em confuse 'em type attack. Their defense is giving up 393 yards a game—giving up 254 yards a game average rushing and 139 yards passing. They are giving up 21.2 points per game. Defense, to their credit, has recovered 11 fumbles, four interceptions.

What Must Be Done on Offense.

> Two important things: 1). Ball control—eat up yards and time, sustain drives, 75-80 plays. When we leave it they must have 80-90 yards to go. 2). Take advantage of scoring opportunities 3 points, 7 points, 10 points does not apply much pressure on them—but 14+ does.

What Must be Done on Defense.

> Turnovers. Fumbles, don't expect them to give them to us, take the ball away. Get the contact fumbles. They

have only lost four fumbles, right? Well, Oregon had only lost eight and you legally caused and recovered seven. Interceptions, as much as they throw I predict we'll get our hands on at least five balls. We must make the catch—we have got to. If we play flawless zone coverage, we can get five. It will also require great pressure (on the quarterback). Kicking, we simply must win the kicking game all phases. Kicks coverage—scoring. No verbal abuse. No media abuse. I don't want penalties. I don't want fights. I would like to turn this game into a classic: A classic shit-kicking!

You have 48 hours to ask yourselves these questions again:

1). Why not play better than you are?
2). Why not hit harder than you ever have?
3). Why not try harder than you ever have?
4). Why not eliminate every mental mistake?
5). Why not wipe everything from your minds but football for two days?
6). Think about how you would perform in the Rose Bowl.

Men, this is our second Rose Bowl Game!

Joe Steele's 83-yard touchdown run and Nesby Glasgow's 73-yard scoring punt return blew open a close game in the final period to spark a 45-21 victory that brought our Rose Bowl vision into closer focus. Our momentum was building, but we faced major obstacles, including UCLA and USC, to win the conference championship and reach Pasadena.

'As a Man Thinketh, So Is He'
October 20, 1977

In his Thursday speech before we hosted Oregon State, James once again insisted that all Huskies maintain a positive attitude. This is perhaps his best speech on the power of the human mind to control thoughts, attitudes, behaviors, and athletic performance. Moreover, it directly addresses the importance of maintaining proper respect for the opponent. Borrowing from the book *I'm OK, You're OK* (Harris, 1967), James urged us to believe in ourselves, respect the opponent, and focus on attaining our goals.

> Modern psychiatry says that there are 4 basic "conditions" of the mind:
>
>   1. I'm not OK—You're OK.
>   2. I'm not OK—You're not OK.
>   3. I'm OK—You're not OK.
>   4. I'm OK—You're OK.
>
> All of these things relate perfectly to a team.
>
> In Category No. 1, we all know people—adults—in this category. It is the invariable condition of the immature, those lacking confidence and the small child (5 years old and younger). In Category 4 is the invariable condition of the complete adult mind—the state of mind of this ball club collectively going into our last two games (big wins over Oregon and Stanford).
>
> Obviously, categories 1, 2 and 3 are bad, bad, bad in football. Categories 2 and 3 show someone who is deeply superficial. Because everything is relevant, deep conditions of the mind are also comparable with superficial or day-to-day conditions of the mind. Category No. 3, "I'm OK, You're Not OK," will lead to upsets like Syracuse. Category No. 1, "I'm Not OK, You're OK," can lead to losing, miserable lackluster performances, and sure defeat because the team is intimidated.
>
> Obviously the desired state of total team psyche in football is just what we have had for two weeks: Category No. 4, "I'm OK, You're OK." With this approach, the team possesses confidence and has that healthy respect for the opponent. This, of course, does not guarantee a win, but it does guarantee "maximum mental state."

Now we know we're OK, what makes Oregon State OK? They beat Syracuse—we did not. Failure to kick a field goal late in game cost them a victory to Arizona State 31-33. They tied USC in the fourth quarter—lost 17-10 to the No. 4 team in the nation! They defeated BYU—No. 12 nationally ranked—their only defeat. Their offense has stopped turning the ball over!

Thinking again about where we are at this point and time of our season. Where do we want to be—want to go?

Following are some Thoughts to Build On:
- From the Bible: "As a man thinketh, so is he."
- William James: "Belief creates the actual fact."
- Buddha: "All that we are is the result of all that we have thought."
- Emerson: "There is no thought in any mind, but it quickly tends to convert itself into power."
- Henry Ford: "Whether you think you can or can't, you're right."

There have been a lot of interviews—publicity—ink—people telling us how great we are. Don't believe it! Remember last week—the reams of paper (positive publicity) about Stanford? "King Stanford has arrived. Greatest victory ever. Great balanced offense, best running game in years."

Here's the Problem with Believing Media Stories:
1. Softens the subjects.
2. Strengthens opponent.

The better we get, the more our opponents build respect for us and the harder they try. Remember: "We're OK—They're OK." Let's show them who is the best!

We did—beating a tough OSU team 14-6 to remain undefeated in conference play. Warren Moon threw a 38-yard touchdown pass to Spider Gaines with 6:40 left in the game and Cliff Bethea intercepted a pass to kill the Beavers' last-ditch scoring drive. However, we lost at UCLA 20-12 the following Saturday, which complicated our dream of winning the Pac-8 Championship and going to the Rose Bowl. Hope remained, however there was no margin for error by the Huskies.

'The Need to Win' at No. 17 California
November 3, 1977

In his Thursday speech before we took our 4-4 record to Berkeley to battle No. 17-ranked California, James underscored our absolute "Need to Win." This speech also offers an example of the life lessons James provided to his players—a theme of his Thursday speeches.

First, James summarized the conference race as a virtual four-way tie between Washington, USC, UCLA and Stanford.

"If we can win three, we can become champions," he said. "It will require our very best."

Secondly, James addressed the strengths and weaknesses of the Golden Bears and mentions that some had accused Cal of dirty play. James said there was no evidence to support the accusation and brushed it off.

"In reflecting back on our past two games," James said. "I can't recall any dirty play so I just assume they have a few gutter mouths that give the team a bad image. Again we're not going down there to debate or fight them."

California has shown steady improvement, he said, citing statistics to show the Bears would be no patsy.

As usual, James had some media motivation for us. "The media in the Bay Area say we're overrated," James said. "They say we're 'not a legitimate contender.' We'll see."

Then James presented the core of his speech, three pages of which he had—unusually—typed:

The Need to Win!

After living through the last six days, one would have to admit:
- We need to win.
- We need to scream and holler and be answered and be proud again.
- We need to see the Purple and Gold of the Huskies dominate an opponent.
- We need to hear the Victory March and know that it is saluting great effort, not just another game.
- We need to return to Seattle and find signs that represent accomplished goals instead of broken dreams.

We had been cocky when we probably should have been apprehensive. We risked psyching up when we knew that awful sensation of falling flat. We had dared to speak of victory when one afternoon of competition could almost destroy us. And somehow, as the new week wears on and we prepare to make this past weekend's defeat the cornerstone for attaining greater heights in the games and years to come, some quieter thoughts reveal an often-overlooked fact.

There was something for all of us to experience during the past weekend. Something about living and life itself. Something about throwing our whole selves into life—even at the risk of disappointment. Even at the risk of failing. This is what life is all about. There's something about seeing life as offering the chance to be a part of a great victory. But offering no guarantees. And there were no guarantees offered to any of us prior to Saturday's game. No assurances that all of the anticipation would be rewarded with painful disappointment rather than great joy. And yet, we all took the risk, we hopped in, feet first, and submerged our whole selves with all of our visions of success. Alumni, students, townspeople along with the coaches and the athletes. Which not only says a lot about our willingness to risk disappointment for the sake of possible success, but also about the ability to trust our feelings with the abilities of others.

In the past we have proved to ourselves that we can achieve tremendous satisfaction if we dare to get totally involved, and we added the comfort of knowing that others can be trusted with helping us achieve that satisfaction. We need to regain that trust in on another. The line for the backs and the backs for the line. The defensive rush for the coverage and coverage for the rush. The blockers for the kickers. The kickers for the coverage. But, we need that every day, we need to be reminded that without this mutual trust, we cannot function as one. All of us involved, all of us together. Every one of us can learn these lessons from the game held last Saturday. But, to leave those lessons on the game field would be tragic. These are great lessons of life. They can help us forever!

Let's not confuse a realistic outlook with a defeatist or complacent one. Let's celebrate our abilities rather than our shortcomings. Let's remember that we can place trust in others to do their job, but only once we have realized our place in the overall plan. For it wasn't only the team that suffered from last Saturday's defeat (to UCLA) in the Coliseum. Every person that cheered for the U of W, every person that risked the heartache, threw himself into the frenzy of competition, they suffered also. Therefore, we can all share in the experience and grow from it and prevent it from ever happening again.

To emphasize his remarks, James wrote the following points in upper case.

Our Needs

- WE NEED TO BE ABLE TO DREAM AGAIN OF VICTORY.
- WE NEED TO BE ABLE TO TRUST AGAIN IN EACH OTHER.

- WE NEED TO GET INVOLVED AGAIN.
- WE NEED TO WIN AGAIN.

They say we're not legitimate contenders? We'll see. Remember, we can place trust in others to do their job. But only once we have realized our place in the overall plan.

1. Master your plan.

2. Then place your trust!

Oh! One last thing! Don't forget the water balloons! I've never been there without seeing our team peppered with water balloons from their distinguished student body. It will make you want to go in the stands and beat hell out of someone. We'll just have to take our frustrations out on Cal's team.

Senior quarterback Warren Moon ran for two touchdowns (one and 12 yards) in the third quarter and linebacker Michael Jackson intercepted two passes to key our 50-31 victory and provide us with a share of the Pacific-8 Conference lead. We trailed 21-17 at halftime before scoring 21 points in the decisive third period. In one of his best games as a Husky, Moon set up the first two scores with long passes.

We Know Who Wins Big Games

November 10, 1977

Coach James was brief in this Thursday speech before the 5-4 Huskies prepared to battle No. 14-ranked USC to keep alive our Rose Bowl aspirations. USC, loaded with talent once again, stood in the way of our Rose Bowl dream. We had many great players, too, and had won four of our past five games. This Husky team included future NFL players Blair Bush at center, quarterback Warren Moon, who would enter the NFL Hall of Fame, defensive back Nesby Glasgow, offensive tackle Jeff Toews, defensive linemen Dave Browning and Doug Martin, linebacker Michael Jackson—among other great players. Plus, the game was in Husky Stadium. As a sophomore on this team, I believed we would win this game—even before James' speech.

USC Game

I don't feel a great need to stand up here and tout this USC team. You know it! I don't feel a need to urge you to try hard. You will! I don't feel a need to attempt to motivate you. You are! I will make a few comments about how and what I feel. The greatest thrill of competitive athletics is to get to where we are right now and to keep going. Most games are won by those with superior talent.

The opportunity for greatness? I believe, and have said many times, that games will usually be won by the more gifted teams. The greatest collection of talent. But I don't believe that about "big games"—contests that count the most. I believe the majority of those games are won by the team that wants them the most.

Last week's game (at California) was a good example. After the first quarter—you can look at our film—it appeared that we might get killed. But we wanted it more. You wanted it more! We saw to it that We, You, got it! (We won 50-31.) California's game with USC the week before was the same. USC was better, but Cal wanted it more.

I think this is our Edge, we must want it more. This way we will fight for every inch of territory. It should be that kind of game where each play must be played with such an attitude that each play will determine the outcome. Then we tabulate the plays. We, with the majority of battles won, will win the war.

The Stats. In six of eight major categories—team ratings—it's USC & UW together. Granted, they are above us on most, but we are the only team in our league consistently close. In individual categories, we are ahead of them in 6 of 9 (categories)—

include kick returns and we're ahead of them in 7 of 11. This points to a little more equity than most people would like to believe. Outside our select group of team, coaches and fans, no one is giving us a chance—pollsters, sportswriters. Head Coach Rich Brooks of Oregon said, "USC and UCLA are the strongest teams in the league and the championship will be decided at the Coliseum Nov. 25" (when the teams meet). Stanford's (Coach Bill) "Walsh casts his vote for Trojans."

James then reminded us of the previous season before the USC game when a sportswriter asked if the Huskies would be satisfied to be competitive against the Trojans, and make USC work hard to win.

I told him "Hell No! There was no place in our program for that kind of thinking." I told him, "Our sights are set on becoming the best and in order to become the best you have to beat the best."

James then read from a story in the *Los Angeles Times* calling USC a "cinch" to win.

Why show up? The L.A. Times already says USC is too much of a cinch. So we might as well forget it, men, and go back to our needlework on Saturday.

As usual, James concluded his speech emphatically.

Men, we just have to want it the most. If you feel as I do you will never want anything any more than a Pac-8 Championship right now. It's ours for the taking. Let's Go Get It!

On a cold, blustery, and wet day in Husky Stadium, we took it all right, beating the Trojans 28-10 and moving another step closer to the Rose Bowl. Warren Moon scored on runs of 2 and 71 yards and tossed a 19-yard scoring strike to Spider Gaines to lead the way before 59,501 fans. The opportunistic Huskies recovered three fumbles, blocked two punts, and intercepted three passes. While the race for the Rose Bowl would be jumbled, we nevertheless had to beat the Cougars of Washington State the following Saturday—in Husky Stadium—to keep our rose-colored dream alive.

Apple Cup, 1977: One Final Step to the Rose Bowl
November 17, 1977

In his Thursday speech before the Apple Cup, James took time to honor our seniors before he explained the enormous stakes involved in this intrastate rivalry for the No. 19-ranked Huskies.

> This Game
>
> Obviously, it's another big game. As you win one the next one takes on even greater meaning: state championship, Northwest championship, conference championship, a TV game, bowl appearance. We may possibly get our game against UCLA in the fall (Sept. 9) on national TV. For the Cougars, it is equally important. We will therefore be playing a good team at their best. What I said last week, I believe: Big games are won by the teams that want them the most. You wanted that game last week more than USC did.
>
> Playing this game will be no different than any of our championship games and will require a flawless kicking game on our part. We must win this phase of the game. You know by now the great contribution our kicking game has made. Last year, the blocked punt for a touchdown vs. the Cougars helped turn the game around. Offense: It would be great if we can control the ball but it's even more important to get points. Field position is extremely important!
>
> Defense: They have a good offense. We've got to fight to keep them off the scoreboard. Force turnovers. (WSU quarterback Jack) Thompson said, "Bring on the dogs." They're coming in here riding high and spouting off. Let's stick it to them. It's just like I said here six weeks ago before the Oregon game: If we expect to compete against California,

Stanford, and USC, we sure as hell have to take Oregon apart. Now it's the Cougars—a good team, yes, but no Michigan or Ohio State University. We must let nothing or no one stop us.

James said diligent film study and focused mental preparation and visualization work would make the Huskies a great team against WSU, and encouraged us all to be vigilant in those areas.

Warren Moon tossed three first-half touchdown passes, including two to Joe Steele (who also scored on a 3-yard run), as we beat the Cougars 35-15 and finished the season 7-4 overall and 6-1 in the conference—losing only to UCLA in conference play. The win gave us sole possession of the Pacific-8 Conference lead with a 6-1 league record. However, UCLA also had only one conference loss, to Stanford, and still had to play USC the following Friday, Nov. 25. The Bruins would go to the Rose Bowl if they beat USC, and we would go to the Bluebonnet Bowl. A USC victory over UCLA would send us to the Rose Bowl for the first time in 14 years. In a close game in which the lead changed several times, Frank Jordan kicked a 38-yard field goal with 2 seconds left to lift USC to a 29-27 victory. For the first time since 1963, the Huskies were headed to the Rose Bowl—the first of six Rose Bowls for the James-led Huskies.

Rose Bowl Triumph

While getting to the Rose Bowl was a huge accomplishment, our dream would be incomplete without a victory. We desperately wanted to beat Michigan, 13-point favorites, and make a statement that the Washington Huskies could beat any team in the country.

Led by Warren Moon's passing and running and two game-saving interceptions in the final 2 minutes by linebacker Michael Jackson and cornerback Nesby Glasgow, we upset the No. 4- ranked Michigan Wolverines 27-20 in the 64th Rose Bowl game on Jan. 2, 1978.

Moon, who ran for two touchdowns and passed for a third to become the game's most valuable player, summed up after the game the great distance our team had come that season. In doing so, he reiterated the messages of dreaming big and faith in each other that James emphasized in his Thursday speeches.

"When we were 1-3, our fans, the rest of the fans in the Pacific 8 Conference and the whole country had given up on us," said Moon, adding the win reflected the confidence we had in each other. "We proved today to ourselves and everybody in the nation that we can play competitive football with anybody. That was my dream and the team's dream—to win the Rose Bowl."

James said he had never seen this team play better.

"We didn't play perfectly, but we played as well as I think we can," said James.

Before a crowd of 105,312, Moon scored on a 2-yard run in the first period and a 1-yard run in the second quarter and threw a 28-yard touchdown strike to Spider Gaines in the third period for our final touchdown and a 24-0 lead, which included a Steve Robbins' 30-yard field goal in the second quarter.

James said the turning point was Moon's pass to Gaines that capped a 97-yard drive after we had stopped Michigan on fourth down at our 3-yard line.

"That was a great defensive stand," James said. "That really gave our team a lift."

Michigan quarterback Rick Leach's 76-yard touchdown pass to Curt Stephenson put the Wolverines on the scoreboard with 4:31 left in the third quarter. Robbins added an 18-yard field goal for us in the third period before Michigan back Russell Davis scored on a 2-yard run early in the fourth quarter and Leach tossed a 32-yard TD pass to freshman tailback Stanley Edwards with 3:44 to play to end all scoring.

A Dream Come True

From a personal perspective, my prayers and hard work were answered when I started out my sophomore season off the Scout Team and on the varsity travel squad. Finally, I was playing in games for the Huskies. My wildest dreams came true later that season when I got to play in the Rose Bowl. The joy was sweet considering the difficulties we endured as freshmen. You see, most of us freshmen toiled as human blocking and tackling dummies on the Scout Teams, running plays for our first- and second-team offense and defense. Among the few exceptions in our freshman class were Doug Martin and Joe Steele who played immediately on varsity.

Getting pounded day after day by Washington's top offensive players wasn't easy, but we created some fun by making plays whenever possible, which drove our offensive teammates nuts because they would then have to repeat the plays until they performed them to the coaches' satisfaction. I knew the only way to get moved from Scout Team to varsity was by making more and more plays in practice. Needless to say, the prospect of tackling fullback Robin Earl, a 6-foot-5-inch, 255-pound bull of a runner—who would go on to make a living as an NFL tight end—gave me pause at first.

I remember talking with fellow freshman Mark Lee, a cornerback and one of our fastest players, about getting off the Scout Team. Lee, who went on to play many years in the NFL, said he had too much talent to be on the Scout Team. He was right, of course, and the coaches finally agreed, too, and pulled him up to varsity later our first year. We freshmen formed a strong bond that helped us endure. Coach James spoke frequently of the importance of goals. My personal goal was to do whatever it took to make the varsity travel squad as a sophomore and play in games. I was fortunate to do so, earning three varsity letters and eventually starting as a senior.

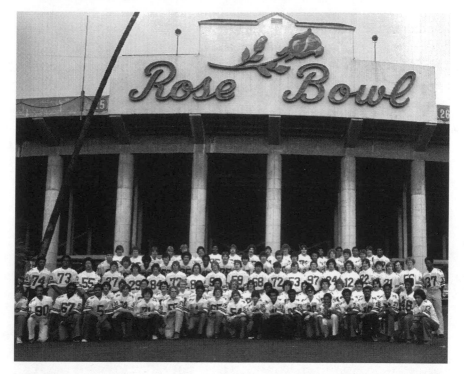

We made our dream come true. The 1978 Rose Bowl team.   *UW Photo*

A Rose Bowl Memory

I was on the Huskies' kickoff team and we kicked off to start the 1978 Rose Bowl. Starting from almost exactly in the middle of the field, next to kicker Mike Lansford, I sprinted as fast as I could to get past Michigan's first line of criss-crossing blockers, thinking I'd cleared them all when wham! I got drilled in the ear hole of my helmet by Walt Downing, the Wolverines' All-American center. Downing knocked me off my feet but I was able to pop up and tackle running back Harlan Huckleby, inside the 20-yard line, a "plus" play in the Huskies' grading system. Maybe it was the shot I took to the head. Perhaps it was the sudden realization that I was actually playing in the Rose Bowl. Whatever the reason, the experience of making the game's first tackle and hearing my name announced in the Rose Bowl Stadium was a real thrill—rivaling the joy of getting married and seeing our three children enter the world.

I had dreamed of playing in the Rose Bowl since I first witnessed the spectacle as a young boy. We stayed in a first-class hotel in Newport Beach for the two weeks before the game—taking in sites like Disneyland and Knott's Berry Farm during the day. At night, there was no curfew the first week but Coach James made sure we were all safely tucked in at the appointed hour the week before the game. While he wanted us to experience the rewards of making it to this grand stage, James and everyone on our team wanted to win.

Formed by Football

I was a painfully shy youngster and football helped boost my confidence—but truth be told, I didn't know if I even liked it at first. It was not until my oldest brother Chris came to watch my practice one day, in sixth grade for Our Lady of Fatima grade school, that I began to love it. Chris coached me to "step up" and "be the hitter, not the hittee." I can still recall him saying, "You've got to stick your nose in there, Peter." When I started doing that, I couldn't get enough football. The first-born of six Tormey children, Chris was a great role model to us all. He went to a great career as a Husky assistant coach, including for the 1991 national championship team, and became head coach at University of Idaho and University of Nevada-Reno.

Our dad, Bill Tormey, a successful cattle buyer who emigrated from Ireland to the United States in 1948 at age 24, was amazed at all the padding we wore for football. In Ireland, where dad had to quit school after seventh grade to help support their large family, he played Gaelic football, hurling, and rugby and said there were no such thing as pads.

"We were lucky if we got a jock strap," he said.

I found Dad's advice on how to avoid injury especially helpful.

"Just hit the other guy harder than he hits you and then you won't get hurt," Dad frequently told me, Chris, and our brother Billy.

Peter Tormey, the author, at UW in 1976. *UW Photo*

Born a month premature at five pounds, eight ounces—Dad said I was about the size of a capon—I was invariably the smallest boy in my grade school classes and was particularly worried about the contact part of football. Discovering for myself that hitting very hard actually kept me safe, football became a source of great joy and the most fun I had ever experienced. I became obsessed with football as a youngster, arising every fall Sunday at 7 a.m. to watch the Notre Dame game highlights from the previous day.

Thanks to football, I became a great reader as well—checking out all the books about football and its heroes that I could get my hands on at the Manito Library. Our dear "Grannie," Edith Tormey, Dad's mother from Ireland, lived with our family for seven years while I was growing up. Grannie and I would walk to the library a few times a month to take back books and get new ones. Mine were mostly about football while Grams' reading tended toward fiction—good literature, mostly, with a wee bit of romance.

I recall the chilly fall day when I set, what seemed at the time, an impossible goal for myself. I rode my Stingray bike to Hart Field, a few blocks from home, to watch Gonzaga Prep play Lewis and Clark High School. I remember being mesmerized by the enormity of the players whose metal-tipped cleats clicked in rhythm like so many tap shoes as the players walked on the pavement from their bus to the field. To me, these guys were like giants, gladiators. I set a goal, then and there, nourished by constant hope and frequent prayer, to somehow, some way play football for Gonzaga Prep. After growing several feet and playing for Prep, I then hoped to play football in college. I was deeply impressed by Coach James and the Huskies and accepted their scholarship over several other schools, even Notre Dame.

Just as Coach James had promised us as freshmen in 1976, during that hot August evening meeting in the Tubby Graves Building, all of our hard work to get to the Rose Bowl and win was worth it. He was absolutely right, the experience is something I have cherished ever since and will never forget. As James said, it all started with a dream followed by faith and hard work. While this sounds simple, the difficult part was persuading everyone on the team to do what James called the "awful" hard work necessary to achieve our goal. That's where his Thursday speeches proved so critical—they persuaded us to believe his vision and inspired us to do the backbreaking work necessary to make it come true.

The First Rose Bowl Creates the Foundation

In a 1997 interview at his home, James spoke of the importance of the 1977 Husky team advancing to his first Rose Bowl.

> General Patton said "to be a good leader, you have to win some battles. If you win some battles, people will follow you

anywhere." That was important what you guys did, getting us to that first Rose Bowl, because if we hadn't done that, we might not have gone anywhere after that, because it impacts recruiting so much, and players' motivation to keep striving. So winning battles is really important. There have been a lot of great generals who have been canned just because they backed out or they don't make the right decisions.

The season after the Rose Bowl, my junior year, we failed to earn a postseason bowl berth, since the Rose Bowl was about the only bowl available to us at that time. In my senior year, we were invited to the 1979 Sun Bowl—a rematch against the University of Texas that we won 14-7. More importantly than two big bowl game victories, however, James said our teams had created a foundation upon which he built a program that culminated in a national championship for the Huskies in the 1991 season.

Success Breeds Success

The 1978 Rose Bowl victory created fertile ground for the Husky program to flourish. If anyone had not heard of the James-led Huskies who upset USC to claim the Pac-8 Championship, there was no escaping the impact of the Rose Bowl success. For one thing, the coaches gained some job security. For another, more of the most-talented football players in the country were choosing to become Huskies.

While winning the Rose Bowl was the most visible sign of success, a more significant change had occurred within the organization's culture, its DNA. In three seasons, James brought the Huskies from obscurity to Rose Bowl champions. To establish a great program, players and coaches had to work even harder—but the path was clear. James' remarkable organizational system and legendary attention to detail became even more focused and refined.

For James, the success added more evidence to his belief in the power of the Thursday speeches and the effectiveness of his approach to the final 48 hours before kickoff. As a result, these elements became more prominent as James sought new narratives to inspire the Huskies.

Unlike many leaders who deliver essentially the same core messages—perhaps in slightly different ways—over and over throughout their careers, James was keenly sensitive to not repeat messages. It was one of the things he worried about most when he became a head coach.

> One thing that I feared most when I became a head coach, because I had heard this from a lot of players, is every time a coach got up, if you played for a coach for five years, you knew what talk was coming. It was "OK, here's the we-got-our-butt-beat talk." Or "here's we're-the-underdogs talk." Or "here's the what-we're-going-to-get in-fall-camp talk." I didn't talk to the team before every practice and after every practice. When I went before the team, I wanted to have something to say. And I felt like I had to have something different to say.

The one message he very intentionally repeated—albeit in different ways—was the importance of players using the final 48 hours to rest and focus on their mental visualization work.

James' reading frequently constituted a mining exploration for inspiration. He read in much the same way as an archaeologist digs for important clues—believing a discovery to help the team might turn up at any time. Stories, he found, were the most powerful motivational tools available. The best stories, he discovered, not only often lifted the Huskies to victory but caused players to pause and reflect deeply. The best of his Thursday speeches offered lessons players would carry with them throughout their lives.

> I felt like if you had to listen to me for five years it would be nice if you didn't know exactly what I was going to say every time I got up there. I thought the stories, a lot of them, would be good for the players, motivational-type stories. But that was

my fear. I knew in fall camp there were things I was going to do in those night meetings, there were things about field position that I wanted to get through, and the rules, and sideline control, and you don't change that kind of material much over the years. We had to go through that again. We can't screw up that part of the game.

With a master's degree in education and experience teaching high school before he became a college coach, James knew a lot about teaching and applied every bit of it to coaching. To truly communicate with and reach the players, James knew the coaches had to recognize that the players all learned and listened differently. And, like many 18-to-21-year-olds, he knew their attention span could be limited.

We all tried to keep our meetings to 30 minutes and that made it easier I think on the players because you knew they weren't going to sit through an hour lecture, or an hour-and-a-half lecture. You can't get people to concentrate that long. If you'd meet with me for 30 minutes, then you'd break and then go with your position coach and he's not going to keep you over 30 minutes. That way, you think better, you act better.

For James, the Thursday speeches constituted far more than pep talks thrown together at the last minute. They were major tactical tools to sharpen the Huskies' performance and inspire victory. As a result, they had to be compelling, well told, and memorable. He relied on them as the one and only way—after the last practice on Thursday and before kickoff Saturday—to improve players' performance in the upcoming game.

The importance he assigned to the Thursday speeches grew in direct proportion to their effectiveness, and by this time James was absolutely convinced of their efficacy. Believing the speeches could provide the difference between winning and losing, he worked increasingly hard on them—focusing on the rhythm, the sound of the words, and other rhetorical aspects to best penetrate the consciousness of the young men who carried out his grand plans. He allocated several hours of his precious preparation time each game week to writing and editing the Thursday speeches, not settling until he found the right combination and order of words to strike the maximum impact. This underscores their importance to his program.

So convinced was James of the power of the Thursday speeches that he continued to refine them throughout his Washington career. His success in leading the Huskies to the 1978 Rose Bowl victory changed his goals, and to an extent altered the content and purpose of his Thursday speeches.

After this first Rose Bowl, James was no longer just encouraging and inspiring a team to play with confidence and believe in itself. Now, he aimed to lift the Huskies to the next and highest level, the Promised Land of college football: the national championship. As a result, he tried to motivate the Huskies in new ways with more compelling stories. And like a concerned and caring parent, he offered more fatherly wisdom, teaching players valuable lessons to help us throughout our lives.

Part II

THEMES OF THE THURSDAY SPEECHES

—

ATTITUDE

—

Introduction

Attitude was perhaps the most important ingredient in James' recipe for team success and it applied to everyone in the Husky football program: players, coaches, trainers, equipment room personnel, the team doctor—anyone who came into regular contact with the Huskies. James had no tolerance for people with poor attitudes, and he felt their negativity infected the team. He spoke about attitude frequently in his Thursday speeches.

"Attitude was the thing that drove me nuts," James told me in an interview. "A poor-attitude kid, I didn't want to be around him. I didn't want to be around poor-attitude coaches." James said he believed, and he wanted everyone on the team to believe, there was no ceiling on the Huskies' success. Through stories and language, he transformed players' indifference, negativity, and fear into confidence.

Following are excerpts from his Thursday speeches, listed chronologically, that focus directly on the importance of attitude.

Two Men Looked out from Prison Bars; One Saw Mud, the Other Saw Stars
October 25, 1979

I feel incredibly fortunate to have witnessed the following Thursday speech before we traveled to play UCLA. I love this talk for its rhyme, meter, and clarity in conveying the truth that we choose, through our thoughts and attitude, whether to live positively or negatively.

This speech led to James' first victory over UCLA Coach Terry Donahue. Washington beat UCLA 17-13 in 1975, James' first year, but Dick Vermeil coached UCLA at that time. Donahue's Bruins had beaten the Huskies in 1976, '77, and '78. (UCLA forfeited its 1977 win due to an NCAA violation.)

After breezing through his general comments and itinerary, an inspired and clearly irritated James gets to the point:

> Generally speaking, people (and football teams included) fit into three groups: Those that make things happen! Those who watch things happen! Those that wonder what happened! If you're on the travel list, make sure you're in the first group—those that make things happen.

James then makes it clear that the Husky players from the Los Angeles area would be allowed to see their family and friends—after the game, not before; no exceptions.

> One other point, while we're on that. Twenty-three of you are from California. Donahue has commented on at least two

occasions, publicly, "We are not losing California recruits to Washington. The ones they are getting, we did not want. Besides, I, Terry Donahue, have not ever lost to Washington." He's right, for three straight years! He enjoys bragging about it.

James reminds us of what he told us on Monday of that week, that players exert either positive or negative leadership, and that he would not tolerate the latter. At this point, he introduces his story about the importance of attitude.

Along those same lines, there is very little difference in people. But that little difference makes a big difference. The little difference is attitude. The Big Difference is whether it is positive or negative.

Nowhere is that point better illustrated than in this story about a young bride from the East Coast after World War II, who had followed her husband to an Army camp on the edge of a California desert. The living conditions were primitive. Her husband had advised her not to come along, but she wanted to be with him. Housing was a rundown shack near an Indian village. Heat—115 degrees. Wind—sand—days were long and boring. The only neighbors were the Native Americans who spoke little English.

She wrote her mother, told her she was coming home. She received a short reply (2 lines):

"Two men looked out from prison bars;
One saw mud, the other saw stars."

She read the lines over and over and became ashamed. She didn't want to leave—she picked stars. In the following days, she made friends with two of the Indians. She asked one to teach her weaving and pottery. At first, the Indians were distant, but then they sensed her interest was genuine and returned the friendship. She became fascinated with their culture and their history.

Then, she began to study the desert and it then changed from despair and a forbidding place to a thing of beauty. Her mother sent her books about it. She studied and learned about the cactus and Joshua trees. She collected shells left millions of years before when sand was the ocean floor. She later became such an expert on the area that she wrote a book about it.

What had changed? Not the desert. Not the Indians. Simply by changing her own attitude, she had transformed a miserable experience into a highly rewarding one. Men, we want and need a positive attitude. We want and need positive leadership. We can readily transform a miserable experience into a highly rewarding one (Saturday afternoon). Every game is important—this one takes on great meaning for 1979 success. We've added some additional pressure. I've asked each coach what he thought about our team and came up with this.

What We Need: We need to restore our confidence. We need to perform like we're capable.

We need to not beat ourselves. Skill people—make some mistakes, OK—but make big plays. If each guy does his job we'll win—don't worry about others. Take the game to UCLA, be aggressive. Execute. Limit critical errors. Don't question others—have faith in them. Defense: Assume every play is coming at you, make plays and be disciplined.

Terry Donahue "King of Washington." We need to correct this. We can do so with a good first quarter, start fast. We can do so with defensive leadership—force turnovers. Respond well in pressure situations. Last year, they defeated us on national TV. There's not a person in America who thought UCLA was better than us. A lot of people will be watching or listening to this one.

We must recover our pride. Let's use the revenge factor—we've suffered two weeks but going on four years as far as UCLA is concerned. Men, this is our championship. We must get totally prepared. We need: Emotion. Excitement. Abandon. Poise. We need a greater commitment than ever. We need to win!

We beat UCLA 34-14. Junior quarterback Tom Flick, in his first start of the year and his second at Washington, connected on 11 of 17 passes for 129 yards and two touchdowns. Mike Lansford kicked two 25-yard field goals and cornerback Mark Lee returned a punt 62 yards for a touchdown. None of us was cheering in the locker room or on the plane ride home, however. Our brother, senior tailback Joe Steele—the Huskies' all-time leading rusher at the time— suffered a knee injury in the game that would end his collegiate career.

An Attitude that Victory Will Be Difficult
October 3, 1985

James delivered a stirring Thursday speech focused on players' attitudes before the game at Oregon. He told the 2-2 Huskies that they were setting themselves up for failure if they went into this—or any game—thinking victory would be easy. He explained how to handle the inevitable adversity in life.

> We establish proper attitudes about the game we then give ourselves a chance to be successful.

> It's that way in life! Good attitude, good things happen. Bad attitude, we're headed for hard times. We all know bad-attitude people—they just go from one difficulty to another. Prisons are filled with these people. Some in here have bad academic attitudes; you will stay in trouble until you change your attitude! So what kind of attitude must we have?

> We must have an attitude of how tough this game will be— how tough it will be to defeat Oregon! We must have an attitude that they have talent and have impact players that, if not contained, can make big plays. We must have the attitude that

they have a good staff and a good strategy. Last year, their offensive and defensive plans were as good as we faced. So, because of these attitudes, we prepare ourselves the way we should. We respect, and we concentrate.

Why do they play so well against us?

My Opinion! This rivalry means more to them than us! They are jealous of our success! They respect us more than we respect them! They become more determined against us! They play with more intensity than we do! They practice harder! They, no doubt, look at more film of you! Who wins big games? It's a big game for them! Like last week (the Huskies beat UCLA 21-14)—the people that want it the most win big games! From these past games they have gained confidence! They believe they can play with us. This then is where they get their edge. If they can get better than us in these categories it lifts their play. Then, if we don't do these things, you can see how it evens out the two teams.

First there is not a great deal of difference on all Division 1-A teams. So we are here—say at a power rating of 85. Give them a rating of 75. Let's say they win 5 points in total preparation and home-field advantage, they go to a power rating of 80. They will absolutely play their best game of year versus UW. Let's say we then are not as intense—that we get beat in preparation. Say we go to (power rating) 82. The result: the teams are now close to even! Men, that's how upsets occur.

Let's look ahead for a moment. Their schedule and record give them another good reason to let things all hang out—as people say. They are 2-0 in league play. They play us then get a bye—two weeks to regroup. They play California—they can beat Cal. Two non-conference games San Diego State, San Jose State—favored, plus two weeks to get better in both. Arizona—they have played well versus Arizona and can beat them. Then, they play Oregon State—haven't lost to them in

10 years. They play USC in the Mirage Bowl in Japan—and believe they could be playing for championship if they get by us.

Let's get back to our game. I think it's safe to say they have built a hatred for us. You have read their quotes. They have called us everything from inept cowards to cheap-shot artists. I'll guarantee you offensive players, they don't have an ounce of respect for you. "Predictable, un-tough" they have said about you. All the calls and articles about how mad they are, and how ready they are for us. Interview (Oregon Head Coach) Rich Brooks this week said Oregon would rather beat UW than OSU. Read it.

Anger—we talked about it last week. You want to go to the Rose Bowl? You'd better stay angry from here on out. I was disappointed in some un-toughness last Saturday from a couple of you. Couple more in practice—EMBARRASSING. Get your ass with it! Stop fooling yourself! This team is not going any place unless we get tougher as a team, every man!! If you step your ass on the bus, I'm assuming you're coming to play! Come to compete! Come to hit! Emphasis on word you!

We talk about the winning edge in scouting reports. The ultimate goal is victory, and if you refuse to work as hard as you possibly can toward that aim, or if you do anything that keeps you from achieving that goal, you are just cheating yourself—plus a hell of a lot of other people in this room. Extra study, extra determination, and extra effort cover those areas that I feel are keys to success—mental, physical, and emotional. This is make-or-break time for both teams. It's time to lock into what has to be done. Do your job. Block everything else out!

Jeff Jaeger kicked four field goals, including two in the final 3 minutes and 7 seconds, to lead scoring in the 19-13 victory.

Concentration and an Old-Fashioned Battle
October 10, 1985

In his Thursday speech the following week, before the 3-2 Huskies traveled to Berkeley to take on the California Golden Bears, James told the players they control their destiny. Washington and Arizona remained the only two Pac-10 teams unbeaten in league play. James opens and closes his speech with comments about concentration; in between, he focuses on attitude.

The Importance of CONCENTRATION

If we were to move ahead to Nov. 16 or Nov. 23 when we would be playing USC or WSU for the conference championship, think about it, how would you play? This game against California this week is just as big. Coach (Joe) Kapp prides himself in his toughness and his team's competitiveness. They have lost to three teams in our league but he says those three teams all lost their next game—claiming that Cal may have lost the game but won the physical war.

So we begin again with attitude. If that's the way they want to play, great! You guys should love a knock-down, drag-out, old-fashioned battle. Set your attitude! Then do it! We had three attitudes last week for Oregon:

1. How tough the game would be—it was!
2. They have talented athletes—Miller, Cherry, Barnes—and they were!
3. Good strategy. They had a good plan with two tight ends.

You would have to agree that these three attitudes were all true. This week! Three More Attitudes!

1. The game will be tough and physical—they are saying that.
2. Respect for Cal as the most improved Pac-10 team.
3. We will get their best shot. We've become a target and this will happen every week.

So we set these three attitudes firmly in our mind, and: We will not be surprised when they occur, and we will be prepared to deal with them. We talk so much in athletics about concentration. I've talked to you about teams that travel, and how a lot of times they don't play as well because they don't concentrate as well—outside influences take their minds away from the game. We could detect in many a difference in the way you played, mentally, vs. UCLA in comparison to Oregon.

Well this week an article was published in the Washington state coaches magazine on concentration, and some of you received copies. Coaches yell it! Concentrate!! But what does it mean? Receivers—keep your eye on the ball. Everyone—keep your minds as well as your eyes on the ball or the key, the play, etc. The point is you have to concentrate continuously, regardless of the opposition, the officials, the crowd, the band, etc. Good concentration does not allow these distractions to creep in and take away from your total effort. Perfect concentration would mean that those things don't even exist.

Concentration also means sustaining an undistracted focus on your goal, whether your goal is immediate, like catching a long pass, or if it's an extended goal—as in season goals. Concentration is like a trance (game face)—it gives an advantage of speeding up learning. It improves performance by making things more automatic. Rick Redman—an All-American here and All-Pro—says it slows the game down for you. Concentration is a learned skill.

For the next 48 hours you will relax, get your mind on your job. Visualize—don't allow your mind to wander. Time yourself—how long can you stay on a subject? Another way is just learning to pay attention to the coach on the field, hear everything your coach says. Look at him. The better you get at that, the more effective you will perform. We always are asked in our evaluation of players—is he coachable? The pros are asking us this question about seniors! I'd like to close with this:

The Label of Excellence. There is no "best" team at midseason. There are only good teams with strong desire who develop their talents and become better. They work and work, even though it may seem like drudgery, until they deserve the label of "excellent." They deserve that rare commendation because they excel. They excel above the other team in dedication and sacrifice; they excel in discipline and training; they excel in spirit and concentration. The team that ultimately comes to deserve the rating of "excellent" knows that it must bestow that title upon itself. It will not come from any panel or poll. To be genuine, it must come from the soul of the team.

The Huskies capitalized on California turnovers to score two early touchdowns, and quarterback Hugh Millen led a 79-yard, fourth-quarter drive to give Washington a 28-12 victory.

An Attitude of Mental Toughness, Never Quitting
November 14, 1985

After beating California, Oregon State upset the Huskies 21-20 the following week, on Oct. 19. The Huskies then rallied to thrash Stanford 34-0 on Nov. 2 before losing at Arizona State 36-7 on Nov. 9. In his Thursday speech on Nov. 14, before the 5-4 Huskies hosted USC, James emphasized the importance of mental toughness, of never giving up.

In his general comments, James says the 1985 season has treated USC and Washington similarly.

Our seasons have paralleled each other pretty much. High expectations. Have conference upset. Both also defeated by ASU. Both experienced injury problems. On the surface, not quitting sounds like an easy thing to do. If you aren't in condition, it will be a lot easier to quit. If you haven't sacrificed, it's easy as you have little to lose. If you don't have tremendous pride it's easy to quit, as you lack motivation to win.

One of the most important qualities is a strong mental attitude (toughness) some call it heart, the refusal to ever give up.

There will be times when we lose. If we must lose, lose with pride! How? Go down swinging. Give them our best shot. Then, get up and practice. Let's break that down. Not quitting sounds easy. Some people don't quit by leaving the team. They quit by giving up within. They don't concentrate! They don't try! They just get by! Ride it out another week—in essence they've quit. They take the check and run. Conditioning: It's not a problem for most but some people quit during a game because of conditioning. Sacrifice: If you're not playing up to your potential, then you haven't sacrificed! Rest—nutrition—effort—weights— study film. We have some who are not playing up to their potential—ask yourself, are you? Are drugs, alcohol, tobacco a problem? Maybe sacrifice is your problem. It's not too late.

Pride! If it's not there, then we the lack motivation to win. Our staff was really trying to hit on pride this week. We lost something with two TV games BYU and ASU (both Husky losses). We lost some with our loss to Oregon State. Take pride in beating your man. We've asked you to take pride in winning your individual battles. Beat your man; outperform him! Beat your counterpart. I also asked the staff to do the same—and I am including myself. So, again, if we don't have tremendous pride we will lack the motivation to win. We will accept ASU, BYU, OSU (losses).

The most important quality is a strong mental attitude. Toughness—heart—refusal to ever give up. How does one player play on broken bones and torn ligaments when another can't function with a hangnail or a cold or other minor problem? Some of you get stung with pain and refuse to lay on the ground and let your opponent have the satisfaction of letting him know you're hurt. Jack Lambert (whom James coached at Kent State and became a Pro Football Hall of Fame linebacker for the Pittsburgh

Steelers) was physically tough but mentally more so. He played a complete season with a separated shoulder.

Some go to the huddle, some to the sideline. Some players are more worried about their pain, while others are more worried about the next play. To be successful as a team we must make up for deficiencies. We must become a lot tougher mentally. Sometimes players with less experience, size or strength beat others because they have more mental toughness, attitude and heart. If we have to lose, lose with pride—let people know they were in a hell of a fight. I know three teams that will not point to us as their toughest opponent: OSU, BYU, and ASU don't believe you were.

Review. Sacrifice, pride, mental toughness are keys. On this team, no one quits physically or mentally within himself. What am I looking for? A game face earlier, a competitive mood swing: grim determined. I'm also looking for BIG HITS—we have people here 3—4—5 years who have never had a big hit. This is supposed to be a contact sport. We're supposed to be a physical team.

Now let's make a list of the things that should in addition piss us off about USC. They were the team that took us out of our championship in '84. After the game their players said ours quit! Now we're faced with getting up for the game! What does it mean? What can these Final 48 Hours do for us? They can get us as well prepared mentally and physically as we can! What does preparation do? It means playing harder. It means running faster and being quicker. It means being mentally and physically tougher. It means defeating your man. It means putting on mental weight. We need all of these things to turn this season around. Last thought—win this one and we will have defeated all four California schools this year.

Chris Chandler, a redshirt sophomore making his first start at quarterback, fired a 13-yard touchdown pass to Lonzell Hill with

56 seconds remaining to conclude a 98-yard drive and lift the Huskies to a 20-17 win.

An Attitude of Vengeance
September 18, 1986

In his Thursday speech before the 1-0 Huskies, ranked No. 7 in the nation, hosted No. 11-ranked Brigham Young, James spoke of setting the proper motivation against the Cougars, who pummeled Washington 31-3 the previous season in Provo, Utah. The Huskies were riding high after crushing Big 10 power Ohio State 40-7 to open the season, giving the Buckeyes their worst defeat in 19 years. In this talk, James wrestles aloud with the difficult concept of revenge.

> Thoughts on BYU. I've been asked this week about revenge. I've heard people say they HATE BYU. Last year, they built up a hate against us over a UW Daily (student newspaper) article. I've heard the term ANGER used. All three terms can be used in our preparation and even help us prepare—if used correctly. Let's examine them.
>
> Revenge, what does Webster's Dictionary say? "To inflict damage, injury, punishment in return for an injury or insult." (Punishment is the best word.) "To take a vengeance on behalf of oneself or a person. Retaliate. A chance to retaliate or get satisfaction, as by a return match after defeat in a previous game." The word vengeance can therefore help us prepare! We don't want to inflict injury, but punishment sounds OK. We suffered—let's make them suffer—payback. Insult? Their players did not respect us in last year's game and many insulted us publicly afterward. I suggest let's take our vengeance! Let's retaliate! Then let's show them some class after the game with our remarks.
>
> Hate, Webster's: "Strong feeling of dislike or ill will. Loathe. Despise." We can't justify this in intercollegiate athletics from

the standpoint of building an attitude of hating BYU's players or coaches. In fact, I have a lot of respect for Coach (LaVell) Edwards and his record. But there are some things we can hate! We can hate losing national championship to them in 1984! We can hate last year's score and hate being defeated on TV. We can hate being put down by some of them; what they said you can hate. You've all seen competitive hate and how it has helped teams coming in here—Oregon, Oregon State, WSU. You think their performance isn't helped by hating us? They get so fired up, swear, flying around, hit, give their bodies to beat you. Hate you? Yes! Why? You're successful. They want what you have! So you don't hate BYU players but you hate losing. You hate having lost to them and you don't ever want to let it happen again!

Anger, Webster's: "A feeling of displeasure resulting from injury, mistreatment, and visually showing itself in a desire to fight back at the cause of the feelings. Implies righteous anger aroused by what seems unjust, mean or insulting." Additional words describing the emotion: Rage. Violent outburst of anger, self-control lost. We don't want this. Fury. Implies a frenzied rage that borders on madness. We don't want this. Ire. Show of great anger in actions, words. We don't want this.

Wrath. Indignation, desire to punish or get revenge. OK. I have coached some players, teams that just play angry, mean, tough—take no crap from anyone. Each team has a few—we need a team image of just playing angry, always pissed as the opponent is trying to stop us from reaching our goals.

Men, we have 10 more obstacles (opponents this season). We just need to get them out of our way, one at a time! Anger helps concentration and makes you hit harder, more determined. Take anger against their offense and defense and kicking game! All professional teams throw. Seahawks held

Steelers to 57 halftime yards. People shut them down. Pressure, cover, hit. Shut them down. Know your plan and how it will be effective. When you get a chance to hit a BYU Cougar, hit his ass. Double payback.

If you like competition, you've got to love this week against the most successful team of the '80s. We've got them on our field. A chance to get some revenge. Each week think Personal Record.

The Huskies got their vengeance, beating Brigham Young 52-21, the Cougars' worst defeat since 1973 when they were crushed 52-12 by Arizona State. Quarterback Chris Chandler passed for four touchdowns and ran for a fifth in the rout.

Be Like Caesar's Invading Army
September 25, 1986

Coach James used a slice of history to inspire the players in his Thursday speech before the 2-0 Huskies, ranked No. 6 in the nation, traveled to Los Angeles to take on No. 12-ranked USC. The Huskies were filled with confidence after two big victories over BYU and Ohio State.

I have been reminded about a war fought years ago "on the road," so to speak, when Julius Caesar sailed over the English Channel from Gaul and landed his men in what now is England. He knew he had no other choice but to succeed. To ensure his success, he made an irreversible move. He landed and climbed the white (chalk) Cliffs of Dover and had his troops look down over 200 feet below. His troops saw fire consuming every ship that they had used to cross the channel. In the enemy's country, with the last link with the continent gone, the last means of retreat burned, there was but one thing left for his army to do. Advance. Conquer. That is what they did. They had no other choice!

We are going down to play USC with that kind of resolve. We're not coming home until it's done. It's not going to be easy. In the last 22 years, only one Husky team has won down there! We have no other choice. Let's Set Our Attitudes: What is the purpose of this trip? Answer now, Win! We're not going to fall into a distraction trap! We're going to outhit a tough, physical team!

This is a tough championship game; both teams are in it! There are eight league games for the Pac-10 Championship, and nine games total for the National Championship. Like eight rungs on a ladder, miss one doesn't mean we can't get to the top, but it makes the climb tougher. We came in second in '84 and almost made it back to No. 1. This is the team that cost us both championships that year. After the game, their players called us quitters.

One rung at a time. Each rung is uphill but within reach. Don't even worry about other teams in our league—we will get to them. One step at a time! Other points to bring up, again! Let's get a Personal Record performance. This is the Olympic Stadium. Think of some of the courageous efforts given in this stadium in 1984. Anger—helps our concentration and toughness as Mike Ditka mentioned in the Chicago Bears highlight film "Play with a Chip on Your Shoulder." Make Them Knock It Off!

Enthusiasm—this game, this season just has to mean more to us than to them. In Norman Vincent Peale's book *Enthusiasm Makes the Difference* he says you set goals that you have to reach! A consuming purpose that just dominates you will motivate you and won't let go! Build a fire under that goal. It's called a fire of anticipation. Keep it burning! Reach that goal! Set another! Fresh objectives. We have 11 games, and a fresh new goal each week!

Norman Vincent Peale on being a team contributor, says learn your role. That becomes a need—fill it!

Keep your mind working on assignments. Concentrate—
think—concentrate—think. Learn to communicate—so much
of football is communication. Know people and like them. You
have to listen to people to get to know them. Ask for help, accept advice—coaching. Believe that your job is the most
important job on the team. Have the attitude that "If it is to
be, it is up to me!"

Review. Trip—no distractions. We can't get caught in that
trap. Concentrate—we must use the Final 48 Hours to get better as a team. Enthusiasm—you beat USC here last season.
Anger—chip on your shoulder. We're going down there with
one resolve.

USC upset the perhaps overconfident Huskies, 20-10. Receiver Ken
Henry caught two touchdown passes, including a 13-yard throw from
Rodney Peete in the fourth quarter to give USC its first lead of the game.

The Link Between Attitude and Competition
September 29, 1988

Two seasons later, in his Thursday speech before the 3-0 and No. 16-
ranked Huskies hosted No. 2-ranked UCLA, James discussed the importance of attitude in competitive athletics.

Attitude and Competition
Sports psychologists, psychiatrists, and successful people put
attitude at the top of the list of characteristics of successful,
well-adjusted, happy people! Have a good attitude and things
go well! Poor attitude, things go poorly! For 18 years as a
head coach, when I go over team rules, I say "Have a great attitude and you don't need rules." Most of the problems that I
have to deal with come usually from a poor attitude! Attitude
of irresponsibility—don't care about others! So we want to
work on our attitude! Why? Attitudes change! This is important for our goals of achieving the National Championship,

Pac-10 Championship, bowls, respect. We must have attitude of this game's importance! We must have an attitude of how tough it will be to defeat them! They are good.

What It Will Take to Win
An attitude of total commitment with each person saying "I'm dumping everything into UCLA game and it will be the greatest effort of my career." We must not simply dip our toes in the water, or go in up to our knees, or our waist—we must get totally submerged in our commitment. An attitude of revenge for our 47-14 loss at UCLA in 1987. Did anyone here enjoy that? We need an attitude of playing through pain—"whatever price I have to pay!" We must have an attitude of respect for our fellow teammates, an attitude that "I love these guys and they will damn well get everything I have!"

We must have an Attitude of Each Person Getting a Personal Record on Saturday. As I speak, the Olympics are going on in Seoul, Korea. Many records are being broken. Most athletes are posting personal records! Many that don't even get into the medal count are still posting PRs. Why? Training, desire, attitude all are bringing out the best in these athletes.

Men, this is our Olympics. We will have a full stadium on Saturday, 74,000 people in the stands, a TV audience of millions, 80 percent of the states will be watching. Football fans around the country will want to know the score, the outcome! Writers and TV commentators, radio, wire service—they all want to know. So we must have 100 percent of the men in here having PRs. One key factor in getting PR? Competition. At Olympics, the competition is the world's best. Saturday in our stadium, we face the country's best or second-best. It takes a good opponent to even evaluate—did I really get a PR? A key point in competition: Make every play critical!

We must clear our minds and, like a computer, we in 25 seconds cover everything that could happen—defensive tendencies, tips, alignments, stunts. Poise—keep yourself under control. Be convinced the next play will win the game! Controlled aggression! Figure out who has the ball, then get 11 guys going after it and kick the hell out of the ball carrier—many times—most times will have to kick hell out of someone first to get there—that's what their blockers are for! You have to earn the right to hit Aikman, Bal, Estwick, Farr.

Offense—as I mentioned Monday, we need about nine guys kicking the crap out of their guys so our ball-carrier can get yards and then he too can run over some of their guys. But the key regardless of down or distance is time on clock. We must have an attitude that the most critical play is the next one! We must go in thinking and believing that! Every play—every day—start today.

How to Cope with Big Games! Most events in life are won by the stronger and faster person. Most big events in life are won by people that want them the most! So when millions turn off their TVs, when 74,000 people leave Husky Stadium, after the writers write, the commentators record, the fans rehash, we want them all saying one thing: The Huskies simply wanted to win more than UCLA! Never stop paying a price for greatness—every man until kickoff—play for 60 minutes Saturday.

Trailing by seven points as the fourth quarter dawned, UCLA scored twice in the final 13 minutes to beat the Huskies 24-17. The Bruins finished the season 10-2 with a Cotton Bowl victory over Arkansas. The Huskies, in an uncharacteristically off year, finished 6-5.

An 'I'll Win It Myself' Attitude
October 26, 1989

In his Thursday speech before the Huskies traveled to Los Angeles for a crucial battle against UCLA, James used the term "insurance policy" as a metaphor for preparing properly to win. After two wins to start this season, the Huskies suffered three straight losses (to Arizona, Colorado, and USC) before turning their fortunes around to beat California and Oregon. James shared how the 1977 Huskies won the conference and the Rose Bowl with each man having the attitude, "I'll win it myself."

How Do We Get Ready for UCLA? How do we duplicate the effort Arizona had against them?

We obviously want a victory! But they too want a victory! Teams and coaches look for great wins, dominating wins. Coaching and playing in a game like Arizona had is a dream! What did Arizona do? They out-coached UCLA. They out-prepared UCLA. They out-played UCLA, out-kicked UCLA, out-hit UCLA, and they out-wanted it! That's Total Domination.

Big games are won by who? Teams that want to win the most. For some teams, the outcome means so much that they are willing to take out what I call an "insurance policy for victory." Insurance? There are times when individuals and teams just will not be denied. The game means so much to them. I've coached teams on days like that. Our first Rose Bowl team was 1-3 then: At Oregon, we won 54-0 and it could have been 70; we beat Stanford, 45-21; at California 50-31; USC 28-10, and we had 21 second-half points; WSU 35-15 and 21 points from our first three drives. Guys made big plays! Big plays! Guys did their job and then helped others. They didn't wait for someone else to make the play.

Look at the UCLA line the last couple of weeks—just stand around, never seem to make a second effort. Our line kicked ass at the point of attack and then got another. Each man had an attitude, "I'll win it myself!" When things get tough, every man seemed to reach down for a little bit more! When things started slipping, this group collectively got things redirected. WSU game? No question, get this one over early. Insurance? We have to pay in advance for it! Want protection? Want coverage? Get your money down if you want a victory.

How does this relate to football? You pay for your victory insurance in advance, in the weight-room, you pay for it in your work in the offseason. You pay for it every day in practice! You pay for it on every play! Then you pay for it in mental preparation! It seemed like Arizona damn near intercepted every pass UCLA threw? Why? That's paying the price, insuring victory. They prepared mentally, knew the routes, never got out of position, read the quarterback. Their offensive line was the same, knew every move!

How do you get yourself so you can play like that on Saturday? Insurance—make your preparation so good—live in the video room—absolutely know every move they make. See, you take the guesswork out of your performance because you know. You insure victory through great preparation. I ask you who prepared better last week—UCLA or Oregon State? Do you think it was worth the effort? OSU called it their greatest victory. They took down the goalpost. I want you to prepare as a team for our greatest performance. I want you to go to Southern California this week with the following attitudes: Respect for UCLA—talent, speed, their ability.

The attitude that we are good enough to win. And the attitude that we are going down there to be successful. I want you to expect the UCLA team that played against Michigan, not the one that played Arizona, OSU, San Diego State.

Realize what this game means for seniors, juniors, sophomores, freshmen—to everyone. I would like to read a team attitude that is a combination of determination and anger, competitively pissed off at: Their powder blue. Their arrogance. Their barking bullshit in our tunnel! Want insurance? It's also tied up with explosion! Not finesse, but explosion of our offensive and defensive fronts coming off the ball! This game, like most, will be won in the trenches. Forty-five hours from now I want to see explosion from the Huskies! Running backs and defensive backs—rock their ass. I want to see explosion of our special teams.

Greg Lewis rushed for 112 yards and two touchdowns, including a 10-yard scoring dash with 1:02 left in the game to lift the Huskies to a 28-27 victory. The Huskies rallied after trailing 21-0 as quarterback Cary Conklin completed 20 of 36 passes for 183 yards and two touchdowns.

LIFE LESSONS

Introduction

Analysis of the Thursday speeches shows a clear pattern: Coach James provided his players with life lessons—words of wisdom designed to inspire them in the moment and far beyond their fleeting days of gridiron glory. James frequently imparted fatherly advice to players that had some application to the team's goals but also were principles and strategies for success in life. He told me that one reason he decided to stay in college football, and not move on to the NFL when he had multiple opportunities, was that college football provided a better opportunity to help form young men. The life lessons James conveyed to players in the Thursday speeches address the development of personal character, inner strength, and a mature striving for success and contributions to the common good.

George Washington Carver Says 'Start Where You Are'
November 2, 1978

In his Thursday speech before the No. 20-ranked Huskies hosted Arizona, James told us about the great African-American scientist, botanist, educator, and inventor Dr. James Washington Carver. Carver's perseverance and drive to succeed in the face of great adversity impressed James tremendously.

> Start Where You Are. Over the years I've tried to leave you with thoughts, affirmations—ideas to help you (and they help me, too) get through the tough days and years. Believe me, we all have them. Dr. George Washington Carver said a long time ago: "Start Where You Are." He said, "Start with What You Have and Make Something of It." He said, "Never Be Satisfied."

> Dr. Carver, a black man, was born into slavery in Missouri about 1864. George was eager to learn—he had no money. He washed clothes in high school and did odd jobs to feed and clothe himself to enable him to go to a one-room school near the plantation. Before college, he washed laundry, clothes for a year in Iowa. He attended Simpson College (in Iowa) for three years. He worked constantly. Then he went to Iowa State Agricultural College, where he became the first black student, and, at age 29, he received a degree.

> His genius with plants and soil won him a position as a teacher at Iowa State Agricultural College. Later on, he returned to the South—Tuskegee Institute. In the South, the main crop at that time was cotton. His approach to crops added income and helped save soil. He taught people to grow vegetables and raise farm animals. His teachings improved diet, and reduced illness and poverty. For over 45 years he taught at the Tuskegee Institute.

> Some of his achievements:
> - He discovered how to turn wood shavings into artificial marble.

- He discovered how to turn bark from Poplar trees into manufacturing artificial silk.
- He discovered from sweet potatoes how to derive flour, starch, vinegar, ink, and other things.

The life of Dr. Carver is a great story—the amazing record of the accomplishments of an orphaned youngster who had to make his start in life unaided. It's the story of a man who earned his way by taking in washing. It's the story of a man who, after paying his first college tuition, had 10 cents left. This is a man who did what he said and believed. He said, "Start where you are. Start with what you have. Make something of it. Never be satisfied!" I thought this might be appropriate for us.

You accomplished something last week: A near perfect game (41-7 win at home over Arizona State) against a fine team. We need to make something of it—build on it. Never to be satisfied!

Success—it's always under construction—never be satisfied—start where you are! We face another championship game on Saturday—win it and we get to play another. UCLA's Donahue said Arizona is more physical than us. Let's get ready, men, we need the same mental preparation as last week in these Final 48 Hours. We need the same intensity, the same physical toughness, and the same get-after-their-ass approach. We do that, then things will turn out fine.

Quarterback Tom Porras scored on a 10-yard run and caught a 29-yard touchdown pass from tailback Joe Steele to lead us to a 31-21 victory over Arizona.

Ingenuity a Key to Problem-Solving
October 16, 1980

In his Thursday speech before the 4-1 Huskies traveled to Stanford, James offered a few life lessons on solving problems. Stanford, he said, posed big problems for Washington and James challenged players to set higher expectations for themselves—both in football and in life.

Now in every season and for every champion there are problems, injuries such as we had Tuesday really hurt. Problems of moving the ball against great defenses. Problems of stopping great athletes or offenses. Stanford poses our most serious problem for the season as far as passing goes. They can throw and catch. Walker Burke—president of McDonnell Douglas Co.—believed! He said, "There is no such thing as an insolvable problem. What appears to be an impossible problem is merely a temporary roadblock to ingenuity." The key is ingenuity.

We have an excellent plan. Far different than any approach we have ever taken with California or Stanford. It is relatively simple, which makes it better. We must totally master the basic zone concepts. Mr. Burke has a creed for his company that is also interesting: "When faced with a mountain, I will not quit. I will keep on striving until I climb over, find a pass thru, tunnel underneath, or simply stay and turn the mountain into a gold mine! With God's help!"

Well men, Stanford is our mountain. They are in our way. We have got to find a way over through around. This is our gold mine. In their two defeats they were beaten physically. They were one of the favorites for champion prior to sanctions. This is our chance to prove ourselves.

Let's kick their ass physically.

Chuck Nelson kicked a 25-yard field goal with :02 left to lift the Huskies to 27-24 victory over Stanford. Quarterback Tom Flick drove the Huskies 72 yards in the last 1:25 and connected with wide receiver Anthony Allen to set up the winning kick. Flick finished with 278 yards and two touchdowns. Sophomore quarterback John Elway led Stanford.

The True Meaning of Fun
November 12, 1981

In the following Thursday speech before the Huskies hosted No. 3-ranked USC as 9-point underdogs, James underscores the crucial link between hard work and success. James takes his cue from a letter he had received a few years earlier from a UW student questioning why the Huskies had to work so hard, all yearlong, in every season, and then even harder during football season. The student questioned James' approach and noted it took all the "fun" from football.

> Letter from a student in the early years of the James Gang, questioning whether our players are having fun. Let me say first that to have real fun in life one must first work. You have come to a competitive university. It's tough in school here. It's tough in football—your staff on average works 12 normal days each week. We all work hard because we are trying to be the best—blood, sweat and tears. This is not like high school—it can't be. But what you get out of it will be fun. It's enjoyable. Victories, a college degree, good grades. You get the satisfaction from doing a tough job well. Is it exciting playing USC? Is it exciting playing before a packed house? When we all work hard and we together can accomplish something great. Is that fun? Yes!

> Then, after you accomplish it, you get to enjoy it for the rest of your life. Our UCLA defeat last week (31-0) was awful—and we have suffered for one week. Now, we can have some fun. Let's not try to make life something it isn't. Let's get what we can out of it. But let's enjoy this association. Note about the student questioning whether we are having fun. Let's talk about that for a moment. The first things we must do are work—not fun. You study, you go to class, fun? But getting a degree from University of Washington is. You practice, it's tough, fun? Some of you enjoy it! Some don't! Our whole football staff was disappointed, like you, last Saturday. Think about the staff and whether they are having fun—they are

working 12-day weeks. Having Fun? Playing USC, is that exciting? Is playing USC having fun? I've experienced three victories against them. Fun? You bet it's fun! You whip USC and you'll never have more fun and enjoyment in your life! I'll guarantee it!

James then speaks to the race for the conference championship before turning his attention to USC.

We've played them in six games, won three. They are the most publicized team by far in the West. People write about them because they've won. You won't find any weaknesses on their team—strong, fast athletes at all positions. I personally like Coach Robinson—good coach, good guy, has class, has won big but has humility. My motivation comes from their tradition! Their record! The opportunity this game presents for us! You don't get many opportunities to play the best. Realistically, not many teams can become the best because you have to play them, and defeat them. We have them on our schedule! We have the ability to do that! We have the opportunity to do that! There's no mystique about them. They just play hard-nosed football. Blue steel—two-fisted contact. That's what it takes.

Further Thoughts on This Game. My purpose for these Thursday meetings is to basically get the minds of everyone connected with the team to begin reflecting on the importance of the upcoming contest and subtle ways that we can use the remaining time to our advantage. There are times when I don't worry. There are times when I have a lot to say! There are times when I have little to say! This is one of those times! Why? I'm not worried. You have prepared well. You got after it real good in practice. You have sufficient respect for the opponent, yet I don't believe you hold them in awe! I do want to talk to you briefly about a couple of points.

Confidence. For an athlete to have a great performance he must have: 1. Confidence in himself! "I can play this game, too. I can whip my man." 2. Confidence in his teammates. This is an ongoing thing—confidence in the line to keep busting their butts blocking for backs; passing, we've got to have confidence to get there with the ball—and then to get it up field. The quarterback has to have confidence to stand in the pocket and not rush, read coverage. The quarterback must have confidence in his protection, that the line will bust their butts blocking. When we rush the passer we have to have confidence taking on double teams. We must have confidence tackling and covering receivers. Our confidence must be strengthened each play of each quarter.

Second Point: Marcus Allen and "the Heisman." He no doubt will win it. I could not care less who wins it as it seems it's just a trophy for a running back on a publicized team. It's supposed to be for college football's best player—it's not. I would just not like to have our team in his personal highlight film. Hold him down. Make him fumble. Keep him out of the end zone. THEY HAVE BUILT THEIR OFFENSE AROUND HIM, CARRY 40 TIMES A GAME!

As I mentioned Monday—no one should be able to carry the ball 40 times against the Huskies! So we have a big challenge. We want to be the best? We then must defeat the best! Have some fun! Create things! Big plays! Light up USC! Light up that crowd! They will help us! Make things happen! You whip USC and you'll never have more fun and enjoyment in your life! I'll guarantee it!

Chuck Nelson kicked two field goals, including one from 46-yards with 2:19 left on the clock, and Fred Small recovered the ensuing kickoff in the end zone for a touchdown to power Washington to a 13-3 upset. As James had guaranteed, the Huskies gained a whole new appreciation for the meaning of fun in the cold, wet, and windy Husky Stadium. Marcus Allen managed 155 yards on 38 carries.

Putting Problems in Perspective
November 3, 1983

In the following excerpt from his Thursday speech before the 6-2 Huskies played at Arizona, James offers six principles regarding problems and solutions—a life lesson for the players.

Now, just a few comments on our problems and solving them. We need to put our problems in proper perspective now with just a few comments on problems and solving them. What is the secret ingredient of tough people that enables them to succeed? It's how they perceive and handle their problems. They look at them realistically and practically. Understand This: Six Principles Involving Problems:

1. Every living human being has problems. Success doesn't eliminate problems; it creates new ones. Example: The better you play, the more you win and the harder people come after us and the more you want to win. A problem-free life is an illusion. It won't happen.

2. Every problem has a limited time span. This is good in that the Arizona problem will be over in two days. The conference championship race will be over Nov. 19 or Nov. 26. The tough part is that we now only have two days to solve the Arizona problem. Don't let problems get you down. Don't let our UCLA loss (the previous week) do it.

3. Every problem holds positive possibilities. Think only in terms of successfully solving the problem. Think only of the positive things that will come from a win this week. Think of the new creative ideas that have resulted from determination to solve them.

4. The facts: Every problem will change you. Every person is affected by tough times. Problems never leave us the way they find us. We have always become a better team after a defeat. Some people—teams—react positively and some negatively.

Our history? Problems make us better—tougher—more determined.

5. You can choose what your problem will do for you! As the saying goes, "You can turn your pain into profanity or poetry." You may not have chosen your tough time, but you can choose how you will react to it. It can make you better or worse. It can make you tougher or weaker.

6. There is a negative and a positive reaction to every problem. In the final analysis, the tough people who survive the tough times do so because they've chosen to react positively. Some people react by quitting, running away, drugs, alcohol—those are negative reactions and may seem to be a temporary solution but they produce greater problems. It's like stealing money to pay a debt—a negative solution; then you're a thief and you're jailed, etc. A positive reaction for us is to simply resolve to prepare better, be more alert, play harder, get tougher and play together.

As big and as important as our first eight games have been, this one is bigger.

The Huskies responded positively to their problem, defeating Arizona 23-22. Cornerback Vestee Jackson broke up a two-point conversion to short-circuit the Wildcats' stunning comeback attempt.

Benjamin Franklin and Virtues for Success
November 1, 1984

In his Thursday speech before the 4-0 Huskies hosted California, James spoke of his great admiration for Benjamin Franklin. He explained Franklin's system to attempt to master the 13 virtues he felt were necessary for success.

First let me remind you of Benjamin Franklin. Benjamin Franklin's story, *The Autobiography of Benjamin Franklin*, is one of the greatest books. Franklin is one of the greatest and most influential individuals the U.S. has ever produced. He was a patriot, scientist, author, diplomat, inventor, printer, philosopher and more. He taught himself to read French, Spanish, Italian, Latin. Through his skill, the U.S. gained independence. He had bad habits like everyone else. An inventor, he worked out a formula to correct his habits. He wanted to do good—be successful.

First he listed 13 Virtues Necessary for Success: Temperance, frugality, moderation, humility, silence, industry, cleanliness, order, sincerity, tranquility, resolution, justice, and chastity. Then, he knew he couldn't master them all at once—so he took them one at a time. He took a small notebook and allotted a page for each virtue. At the close of each day he marked down each error he made that day and kept this up until he had mastered it. This was possibly the first success recorder of mankind.

Additional Thoughts. Let me say that from my talk last week I think you gained some respect and some of the frustration is gone—but it's not gone completely.

James then told the Huskies about one of his favorite books, *The Greatest Secret in the World,* written by Og Mandino. He recommended that every player buy the book "as a guide to success and happiness—you will get many returns on your investment."

James then quoted extensively from the book, including the following excerpt.

"I will never consider defeat and I will remove from my vocabulary such words and phrases as quit, cannot, impossible, out of the question, improbable, failure, unworkable, hopeless, and retreat; for these are the words of fools. I will toil and I will endure. I will ignore the obstacles at my feet and keep mine eyes on the goals above my head. I will persist until I succeed."

I will win! We've been talking about this for 306 days. Get better, do it today, persist. Get stronger, do it today, persist. Get smarter, do it today, persist. Get tougher, do it today, persist. I might add that in the back of this book it lists the 12 greatest books for successful self-improvement. *The Autobiography of Benjamin Franklin* is rated No. 1. Then it lists 10 more. Then it says that if you counted you will find only 11. It goes on to say that No. 12 is probably already in most of our houses—the Holy Bible! If you want to read any of these I have them—all—in my office.

Cal is another obstacle that we must deal with. Darrell Royal, the former Texas coach, said a successful football team must play angry and remain angry. I concur. Let's get after their ass.

The Huskies whipped California convincingly, 44-14, as Jacque Robinson rushed for 152 yards and three first-half touchdowns. The win gave Washington a 9-0 record for the first time in school history.

The Harder We Work, the Luckier We Get
October 2, 1986

In his Thursday speech before the 2-1 and No. 12-ranked Huskies hosted California, James discussed what the team must do to dig itself out of the hole it created by losing the previous week at USC (20-10). James goes on to provide a speech filled with life lessons.

Thoughts on the game: Let's talk a moment about our situation! We talked about the ladder last week—we didn't get to the first rung. We dug a hole that will require some tough digging. We could have stayed undefeated and untied and you would have a little cushion. We are, and will stay in, a must-win posture. We can become conference champions—but now help is needed! We can't be distracted. We can't get fooled. We must concentrate. We can't fumble, etc.

We put our backs to the wall, still there is no need to panic!

But let's realize: If we let them, all of our conference opponents can play! Every team we play will question themselves? Are we good enough? THEY SAY: "Huskies are better! We want to defeat them. We are willing to give everything we have to defeat them, but they're better!" THEY SAY: "We must gain confidence and motivation from staying in there with them early." That's what they say. THEY SAY: "We must take the Husky fans out of the game!" I see this every season—normally from all Northwest teams! Come out fast: Get some early scores and you can name the score.

What now must we do!
1. Get some injured players back. 2. Must remain relatively free from injury! 3. Must build depth. Our back-up players must get better! 4. You must practice your butt off! Be ready! 5. We have eight tough games left but we will concern ourselves at this time with only one. The one that is up next. Let's make our opponents hate playing us. Let's make them pay a price! 6. Be as well prepared as you possibly can. 7. Know your plan! Know your opponent! Every move! 8. If he reacts differently, you immediately know something is up. 9. You must defeat your man!

I'd like to refer to another book: *What It Takes to Get to the Top and Stay There* by Charles W. Golding. He believes there are five essentials.

1. A vision of yourself. See yourself at the top!! See yourself as champions—playing in the Rose Bowl. Believe—no doubt—it's just a matter of a few weeks! Let's keep the part of being champions private, not public! Let's take a little time to dream, but don't become a dreamer! Like last week, set a goal that you MUST achieve! From the time you wake 'til you go to sleep, think champions!

2. Determination (motivators). Some think it's money or fame! What it is is a challenge, stimulation, responsibility, achieve-

ment, satisfaction. Know yourself! What makes you deter-mined? Being a great competitor—a winner.

Dedication. Determination is the fuel of dedication! To pull this championship off we must dedicate our entire being to the sub-jugation of everything else—drugs, alcohol, tobacco. We must rest, watch our diet, lift. Champions will do this. Many will not. How else will we get the energy to reach the top? Remain you—do not change moral values. If we change them to get to the top—we lose! Dedication is not work—it's fun! The challenge provides the adrenalin to get better! We must be willing to work in the trenches, to do the dirty work, get tired, get beat up. You can control your opponent. You can beat your man only with talent. And talent and skills are learned in the ditch!

Let me tell you the story of a swimmer—he read books, pre-pared, went to the coach and asked, "What is it, coach? Weight training? Isometrics? Running? Stretching? I want to really be a good swimmer. Possibly the new dimensional gym? What should I do?" The coach says, "Look kid, you wanna swim? Get in the pool!" I could name at least five football players that failed making a pro team for two reasons: missed a practice or played a spring sport. The players said, "Coach, it'll help my speed or my hand-eye coordination." Bullshit! WE ARE NOT GOING BACK ON WHAT WE TOLD YOU! You have to be dedicated. You have to get in the trenches! Get dirty—get bloody—get better.

4. Ability to risk: Put your job on the line but never in fear. Your actions must be cool, calm and calculated. The actions of a future champion! Get down to a play or drive that has to be made. It's exciting. Why do fans stand up? Why do they scream and holler? Last year in the fourth quarter we were ahead of Cal 14-12 before our offense went 79 yards to go up 21-12. Last year against USC we went 98 yards in 4 minutes. Two fourth downs. That's exciting.

5. Luck. Have read studies that believe that only 2 percent of the people are thinking about and can thus see the opportunities that are presented them. These few people feel lucky! They think lucky! Prepare yourself better and you will be surprised at how lucky you get! The old quote is true, "The harder I work, the luckier I get." That's a great truth!

Review: Dig ourselves out of the hole! One week at a time. Get back on the ladder! What it takes to get to the top and stay there:
1. A vision of yourself as champs.
2. Determination.
3. Dedication.
4. Ability to risk.
5. Luck.

Nothing stands in our way! Make the decision to go for it! The harder we work, the better we get! The luckier we'll become!

Led by their highly opportunistic defense, which intercepted six passes and recovered three fumbles, the Huskies beat California 50-18.

'Faith is Knocking Down the High Bar'
September 24, 1987

In this excerpt from his Thursday speech before the 2-1 Huskies hosted Pacific, James shared some insights from Robert Schuller, a minister and author. James sought to inspire the Huskies after they suffered a 29-12 loss five days prior to Texas A&M.

Faith is Knocking Down the High Bar.

Says Robert Schuller, "Oftentimes faith meets success at the point of failure!" One of the easiest things to lose when we lose a game is confidence, faith. That's why one ingredient to squad development is loyalty! It helps carry us through tough times! Robert Schuller's example is of a pole vaulter who runs and vaults a little higher each time but doesn't know how high he can jump until he fails to scale the bar. Schuller says, "He succeeds when he fails! Failure isn't a matter of not reaching the goal! Failure is failing to give all that you've got" to your team. Each man does his own soul-searching.

Schuller's definition of success is achieving the maximum of your potential in the situation you are in. When you have attempted your ultimate best, then you are successful, in spite of failure. The people who are really the failures are the people who set their standards so low (keep the bar at a safe level) that they never run the risk of failure! Faith is daring to face an embarrassing failure (lose on national TV). It's only after taking A&M on, competition at its highest level (the high bar) that we know we jumped as high as we can—today!

Success then comes because we maintained that faith and trust in each other and the next time that bar is raised we will get over the top. Look at our schedule. We get back into the competition these next three weeks. The bar keeps getting higher:

12 feet—University of Pacific
14 feet—Oregon
16 feet—Arizona State
Then—USC

Review. Failure is failing to give your team and yourself all you've got! Trying to get out of things—failing to go to class, making grades! Do your film study, weight lifting, treatment. How Do We Succeed? Success is achieving the maximum of your potential in the situation you are in. So this week, in a game we are heavily favored to win, we could win the game and fail in the competition by playing sloppy football. We don't want that—it's not our approach, it's not our goal, it's not how we measure success! Let's raise our standards (bar) this week. It's UW playing UW this week!

If we really want to become a great team? Then we break it down by objectives: Kicking game? Reach objectives. Punt return: 10-yard average, hold up your man. Punt cover: Less than 3 yards on return, cover your lane. Kickoff return: Bring it to the 30 yard-line. Cover your lane. Offense? Reach objectives: 35 points, 0 turnovers, convert 50 percent of our third-downs, get five drives with eight plus plays. Defense reach objectives: 7 points or less, get four turnovers. Get field position or score. Prevent big gain. Stop third down 70 percent of the time. Do these things and there will be no question over the outcome. We will succeed. We're better.

Led by junior Aaron Jenkins, who rushed for 107 yards and three touchdowns, the Huskies routed Pacific 31-3.

Wisdom from Vince Lombardi and Helen Keller
October 8, 1987

In his Thursday speech before the 3-2 Huskies hosted No. 13-ranked Arizona State, James described the game as crucial for the season. He offered some life lessons about character from Vince Lombardi and Helen Keller to lift the team after a tough 29-22 loss at Oregon the previous Saturday.

> The outcome of our ASU game is very important to the season. What we want to accomplish for 1987 and we have a lot left.

After going over the Pyramid of Objectives and the strengths of the Sun Devils, James reads a famous speech by Lombardi.

> This is the "Habit of Winning" by Vince Lombardi. "It is a reality of life that men are competitive and the most competitive games draw the most competitive men. That's why they're there—to compete. They know the rules and the objectives when they get in the game. The objective is to win—fairly, squarely, decently, by the rules—but to win. And, in truth, I have never known a man worth his salt who in the long-run,

deep down in his heart, did not appreciate the grind, the discipline. There is something in good men that really yearns for (needs) discipline and the harsh reality of head-to-head combat. But I firmly believe that a man's finest hours, his greatest fulfillment, is the moment when he has worked his heart out in a good cause and lies exhausted on the field of battle victorious."

James then offers the following quote from Helen Keller:

Helen Keller said "Character cannot be developed in ease and quiet, only through experiences of trial and suffering can the soul be strengthened, vision cleared, ambition inspired and success achieved. Face your deficiencies and acknowledge them, but do not let them master you." This is as true for football as it is in life. What incredible greatness came from a deaf, blind woman.

She had no excuses. Born in 1880, at 19 months struck totally blind and deaf. College educated, she set up foundation for the blind. Lectured around the world. In World War II, she worked with soldiers who were struck blind. In her 50s, she worked in Africa to help the blind. She died in 1968 at 88 years old.

ASU

It's the first time ASU has been up here in Seattle in five years. They have the general feeling that their program has surpassed all others in a few short years. They are the team that called us slugs. They have also been quoted as saying we are the most overrated team in the Pac-10. Helen Keller said "Character cannot be developed in ease and quiet, only through experiences of trial and suffering can the soul be strengthened, vision cleared, ambition inspired and success achieved. Face your deficiencies and acknowledge them, but do not let them master you." This has a great deal of truth in it. I especially like the last line: "Face your deficiencies and acknowledge them, but do not let them master you." This is where this program is right now. It needs a great victory!

Why? Two defeats. Negative comments. Comments include, "You can't win the big game." Also, "No Rose Bowl since January 1982." We suffered a defeat by Oregon. We suffered a defeat by ASU two years in a row. We need to get our pride back! We need to regain our respect! It's fun being considered a Top 10 team. It's fun being recognized as a national power. It's great having won the respect of our opponents. But we have to beat someone good! These things will not return by defeating University of Pacific, Purdue, or Stanford. That recognition goes deservedly to the team that can defeat ASU and USC. We're talking competing!

My objective each Thursday is to get every man in here into the game and only the game in the Final 48 Hours. You men in here would have to rate in the top 10-20 percent in a competitors' rating of people across the country. My goal is to get you into the top 2 percent by Saturday.

Motivation for productivity is my main job, getting the most out of the talent in here—coaches and players. Collecting a group of talented people and squeezing the absolute maximum of the potential you have. That what it takes to beat a great opponent in a big game. Compete to our best ability. We have the opportunity—reigning Pac-10 Rose Bowl champs—TV, what better time than now to regain that pride? No one else can knock off ASU this week.

We have had our adversity—when you get it some quit, but winners get better because of it. No one cared much for the Oregon defeat. You picked it up a lot as a group. We had our best Tuesday practice this year by far. Wednesday was good intensity. Most tough competitors take a roadblock and merely make it a stepping stone to success. It makes us more determined. It simply makes us better. It's already making us a better team. Every man and coach on this team knows he can do better—and has done better this week!

As I mentioned in 1980 we lost to Oregon 10-34 in the third game. We had the same frustrations—but our team came back and won every other Pac-10 game to become Pac-10 Champions. History does repeat itself if we make it happen. That team of 1980 was equally frustrated and disappointed but because of the defeat we got a whole lot better.

Back briefly to ASU. They are a very good team. They don't respect our team. They don't respect our program. It's time they do. But we must earn it. Get ready for one of the most exciting afternoons of your life!

The game was exciting indeed, and the Huskies dominated the fourth quarter to whip the Sun Devils 27-14 and regain their pride. Tony Covington scored on a 1-yard run and Brandy Brownlee kicked a 36-yard field goal in the final period to spoil the Sun Devils' Pac-10 Conference opener.

'Realism and Optimism Go Hand in Hand'
September 22, 1988

In his Thursday speech before the 2-0 Huskies hosted San Jose State, James offered a life lesson about optimism and realism.

Optimism and Realism

On Monday, my closing remarks were: "Think about how good we can become. Think about how good we want to become" and "Think about how good we have to become if we are going to win a championship." That's our target!! Our Goal! We must be realistic and optimistic!! Winners are optimistic, they expect to do well! Losers are pessimistic—negative—they see rain while winners see rainbows! I have never coached a team without problems. Let's look at our problems as opportunities!! We have worked to solve problems, and still won! I will closed with the winners' self-talk: "I was good today, I'll be better tomorrow." Don't waste a day men, you can't get it back! Webster's definition of optimism: "Expect the best outcome." Key word is expect! We can do it! We will do it! It's another great day! We/I expect a great year, positive!

To be optimistic: Stay relaxed no matter the pressure or tensions, why? It keeps us confident, optimistic. Ulcers are not caused by what we eat but how we handle stress. Don't participate in group griping—think of something positive to say when those around gripe. Be optimistic! Be positive! Optimists cure the curable, fix the fixable, prevent the preventable. Optimists enjoy the competition and preparation! Optimists have daily personal meetings!! "I'm feeling better! I'm getting stronger! I'm quicker now with rest and nutrition paying off! I'm a lot further ahead than last year at this time!"

Expect the best from your coaches and teammates, give your best! "I'm giving them all I have because I know I'm getting all they have!" Be proud of your teammates. Brag on your teammates' work habits. Realism and optimism go hand in hand.

Ask, where are we? What will it take to get to where we want to go? Let's analyze now some of that realism! Many times we've discussed and compared the first three opponents this year to the second group of four. Only doing this to place emphasis on need to evaluate our performance as a team—the various levels of competition. Fact: We need to raise our performance level. Why concern ourselves with that this week? Because it's important for San Jose State to compete with Pac-10 teams: OSU, UW, California, Stanford. They are a better and more explosive offense than Purdue or Army. Their defense will attack more—pressure more. I've seen films of them in past years putting dogs, blitzes, crashes on California and

Stanford nearly every play. They play pressure defense and man coverage!

Two Concerns. Obvious concern: If we play at the same performance level we could be upset! Obvious concern: If we play at the same performance level, we could be 3-4 after seven games.

So we get our motivation from our optimism and realism. Dream some, win big, champs. Motive? To provide motivation. To move you to action! Back to realism: Approximately 30 percent of the 11 players on the team on the field at a time are playing below a passing grade. Offense, defense and kicking game. Men, we have an incredible obligation to this team, you and I, we have signed on! We have committed ourselves! We can't ask for more than 100 percent. But 100 percent is expected. 100 percent in practice. 100 percent preparation. 100 percent performance. Are we satisfied with our performance in the first two weeks? This has to stop! These poor individual performances must go. We must do our job.

Want a serious question? Question yourself—how many damn games can this team win with me playing the way I have? No more excuses, we've all heard them. "I've been hurt. I'm only a redshirt freshman. It's my first start. I'm playing a new position (four starters out)." People don't give a shit about that. Excuses! That's all they are. What's the bottom line? Profit, loss, victory and defeat! Well, the bottom line on getting better is preparing better. Those of you who have struggled, have you been concerned? I saw some players studying film until 11 p.m., on their own free time. How about you?

Did you spend more time on your opponent? Did you go back and re-evaluate your first two games? The films are sitting there! Since Jan. 1, nine months men, we have been counting the days. Are you counting? Are you milking each day to get better? Well in nine days you're going to face what may be the best college team in the country! Will you be ready? Will we show some competitive maturity by kicking the shit out of San Jose State? Put a chip on your shoulder!!! There's still competition for some jobs. Go win it! Display of toughness—no nonsense. Be optimistic about getting it done! Be realistic about what it will take!

Tony Covington scored on a 2-yard run with 1:31 left to lift the Huskies to 35-31 victory over the Spartans who had erased a 28-0 deficit to move ahead by a field goal with 4:08 left in the game.

Confidence: Your Greatest Reward
October 27, 1988

In this Thursday speech before Washington hosted Stanford, the 4-3 Huskies were struggling to achieve a winning record after three conference losses that had ended hopes for a conference championship. In his previous Thursday speech, before Washington lost at Oregon 17-14, James told the team "to gain motivation from five-week goals." In this speech, James changes the focus to short-term and offers some life lessons on the proper reaction to adversity.

> The focus now is on one day and one game at a time! There is still a lot to be accomplished, a lot that you can be proud of. Now it's not OK to just play someone close. We need a complete victory on offense, defense, and kicking game. Supporters and media have been pretty solid behind us. Let's keep them there with quality football.

After reviewing the strengths of Stanford's offense, defense, and kicking game, James strays from his usual game comments to a different approach to build the team up and redefine success and failure.

> Some Random Thoughts. I'm not trying to convert any of you and I believe in the separation of Church and state. Still, the Bible is the best book ever written on how to live. In Hebrews

10:35: "Therefore, do not throw away your confidence, which has a great reward." Confidence has your greatest reward. Don't surrender to fears. We had such high goals—such high expectations this season. It's important now that we have had adversity to not perform with a fear of failure approach. If any of us have this fear of failure we must cure it! How?

Say this to yourself: "I'd rather attempt something great and fail than attempt nothing and succeed." I admire people who make a commitment! People who stick their neck out put it all on the line! I admire you guys! I admire people who try to reach the top. You were willing to put it on the line against the No. 1 and No. 3 teams in the nation! Whether you make it or not, you are winners! Have you ever seen a team face more adversity in your life than we did against USC and Oregon? Did you see anyone in here quit? Hell no, you didn't because we don't have quitters in here. You fought back. You nearly won!

You see, when you lose you're not a loser unless you quit! There is no need to fear failure. You can become the team you want to become, winners. There is still plenty of time! Pastor Robert Schuller in one of his many books printed this about failure.

James then reads a passage from Schuller, substituting the word "we" for "you" to make it applicable to the group:

"Failure doesn't mean *we* are a failure ... it does mean *we* haven't succeeded yet. Failure doesn't mean *we* have accomplished nothing ... it does mean *we* have learned something. Failure doesn't mean *we* have been a fool ... it does mean *we* had a lot of faith. Failure doesn't mean *we've* been disgraced ... it does mean *we* were willing to try. Failure doesn't mean *we* don't have it ... it does mean *we* have to do something in a different way. Failure doesn't mean *we* are inferior ... it does mean *we* are not perfect. Failure doesn't mean *we've* wasted our *season* (life)... it does mean *we* have a reason to start afresh. Failure doesn't mean *we* should give up ... it does mean *we* must try harder. Failure doesn't mean *we'll* never make it ... it does mean it will take a little longer. The failure *we* have experienced is not final! Or fatal."

We need to stop the suffering, "stop the bleeding." The Denver Broncos' coach says you need to play this game mad. Mad at the turn of events. Mad at the opponents. It's a tough physical contest—so get mad. Chicago Bears Coach Ditka says play with a chip on your shoulder! What does that mean? Basically that "I'm tougher than you are. Want a piece of me? Come on, let's have at it! If you get near me, you're going to get your ass knocked off." The things we have discussed in prior meetings will always hold up. Play with great desire! Play with enthusiasm! Play with emotion! We've played good teams close. Now let's start kicking the crap out of people. You now have 45 hours to sort out how you personally will perform. Let's be accountable! Let's get it done! Let's go to work!

Cary Conklin passed for two touchdowns and Tony Covington and Greg Lewis both scored on 1-yard plunges to lift the Huskies to a much-needed 28-25 victory over Stanford.

With Backs Against the Wall, How to Handle Criticism
October 5, 1989

James offers players some wisdom about handling criticism in his Thursday speech before the Huskies travel to Los Angeles to battle USC. The 2-2 Huskies had lost two games in a row—to Arizona and Colorado. James reminds the Huskies that failures, temporary setbacks, are a natural result of aiming for lofty goals, and he suggests that most critics are pessimists.

Handling criticism is tougher than handling praise—we've had two weeks of both! To completely avoid criticism, you

must: 1. Say nothing—never voice your opinion about anything. 2. Do nothing—don't compete ever, fight for a cause.
3. Be nothing—if you don't try to succeed at anything, you
won't ever fail. So repeat the above to avoid criticism you
must: (1), (2), (3). Quote: Charles Nelson says "a pessimist is
someone who is seasick during their entire voyage of life."
Most critics are pessimists. It is said that when pessimists
meet at a party, they don't shake hands—they shake heads. So
do-ers and positive people are always open to criticism. When
it occurs there are two general reactions to this criticism that
are wrong! 1. Fight back, get angry (I've been guilty of this
many times). 2. Lay down and quit. Many people do—this is
the easiest way to solve problems, back away.

Let's Explore: Fight back. If it's authority, you just dig a
deeper hole. If it's your boss, you're fired. If it's your profes-
sor, you fail. If it's your parents, you're restricted. If it's your
coach, you don't play. If it's someone not important, the anger could cause further bitterness, fights, yes, even killings
(happens daily). Lay down and quit. It's like walking through
life with a parachute on, every time we face adversity or criticism—bail out! Quit. A lot of people do this! The problem is
that you quit once and it's easier to quit the next time. You
become an expert at it!

OK so what is the right way? Know who you are! Like who
you are! Be who you are! Let's Explore: Know who you are:
I'm me. I'm proud of who I am. I've achieved (with strengths,
weaknesses and limitations) a lot. I've done a lot that many
people couldn't do! Accentuate the positive! Like who you
are: I'm making good progress, character, education, athletics. I may not be there yet but I'm making progress—I'm
getting better. I like my chances for a very successful life! Be
who you are: You can have role models, you can work to be
like others you like, admire! But you have to be yourself.
Take pride that you are unique!

Don't be derailed by answering your critics. There are always important things that must be done! Don't let the internal feeling eat up what you should be doing! I've been guilty of this! Now just trash it! Do what you can to improve. Just say, "I don't have all of the answers but I'm doing what I feel and believe to be the best!" Critics try to eat you up from the inside. They are like parasites. They are not willing or never have done a thing themselves. They would rather eat away at others.

Application: When criticism is correct, accept it! "I am wrong." Most unwarranted criticism does not need to be answered. Don't make war every time you are criticized. Let it go on by! When you do need to answer critics, just give the facts as you know them. Let it be done with! We can never lay all critics to rest. As long as we are in the arena, doing things, we're criticized. It's never going to end. Now that we've handled the criticism topic—just remember this will be with us daily—all of our life. Just know how to deal with it.

Now let's deal with USC. How do you win a big game? Want it more! How do you do that? Prepare yourself for the most important game of your life. Be willing to give more of yourself. 1. Preparation. 2. Performance. I said Monday, "explode every time you hit a red jersey." We changed jerseys Wednesday—get the idea. Bill Glass Approach. Bill Glass was a Cleveland Browns defensive lineman. He wanted to give everything he had. He wanted to be carried off the field when the game was over. He wanted to be carried onto a plane if he couldn't bounce back. Basically he wanted to play his best, hardest ever, save nothing. He knew his body would respond after a while. He made a tape recording and played the recorder all night: "stop runs, stop pass, sack quarterback, beat my man, every play!" He said he learned how to compete and what his limits were. He learned that before he did this, he never came close to his potential. He became a consistent All-Pro defensive lineman. Out of college, it was a pretty sure bet that he couldn't make it!

I said yesterday—an exceptional performance is needed. To get that, we need exceptional effort! This is not Mission Impossible! This is Mission Important! We need 60 tough SOBs on this trip!

Todd Marinovich threw for one touchdown and ran for another to lead USC to a 24-16 victory. Like Bill Glass, the Huskies fought hard and gave it everything they had. Washington missed a chance to go ahead in the final period after a 31-yard touchdown pass from Cary Conklin to Andre Riley pulled them to within 17-16.

COMPETITIVE GREATNESS

Introduction

Coach James' concept of competitive greatness permeated the program and is found throughout the Thursday speeches. Codified in the Husky football playbook from the start of the James era, it meant competing at one's utmost capacities in all circumstances. James saw competition as an inherent good that makes everyone better, and improved the entire Husky football organization. He believed "competitive greatness" focused energies on top-priority quality issues. The following excerpts from his Thursday speeches capture his emphasis on the

Huskies becoming the best competitors possible, individually and collectively.

The Dynamics of a Winner
October 4, 1979

James was a student of the dynamics of winning—the factors that contribute to a team's ability to consistently compete at the highest level. He spoke of winning dynamics several times in the Thursday speeches, including this one before we hosted Oregon State.

> The past couple of weeks we've taken key points and placed additional emphasis on them so that we as a team can continue in our quest for 1979 success. Areas that I have felt were extremely important to our progress are: Aggression. Mental Toughness. Always Improving. Still, as we work through the year, we don't simply concentrate on new dynamics and eliminate the old ones. We add to the existing dynamics. We want to get tougher physically and mentally each week. We must improve each day—we are not close to our team's potential.
>
> Desire Factor
> 1. That burning desire and drive that will make us prepare regardless of the situation. The enjoyment of facing a challenge—take that No. 7 ranking out on the field and see if OSU can do anything about it. We talked about stakes! Men—there's a big pot with everything riding. The difference? We've got a hell of a lot more in the pot. They (OSU) can take the greater gamble.
> 2. Want to be a winner—I'm concerned that you do and are willing to pay whatever price it takes to get it done.
> 3. Look forward to competition. I know that you are.
> 4. Set high goals—aspire to be the best.

I bring these things to your attention because there are very visible ingredients to keep us from being successful. Chemical additives are put into water to soften it. Zeolite crystals occur in nature, and can be manufactured, help soften water. What softens us? We have our athletic softeners, our own form of zeolite for this game: Film of OSU shows them in defeat four times. Oddsmakers—saying we are heavy favorites. Newsprint media talks of our soft schedule and negative comments about our opponents. Friends—telling us how good we are. We must then counteract this softener factor and manufacture our hardening chemicals.

OSU is a rival opponent, but is that enough? This, plus personal pride should be enough to harden us to the task. This plus aggression improves drive, helps us become mature competitors.

Is the prospect of a Conference championship enough to harden us to the task? Is the prospect of a National Championship enough to harden us to the task? Is our National ranking of No. 7 enough?

The Huskies, 26 point favorites, were indeed hardened to the task, walloping Oregon State 41-0. Joe Steele scored on runs of 18 and 13 yards while Tom Porras tossed an 11-yard touchdown pass to Paul Skansi—among other scores.

Competition Brings out the Best
October 11, 1979

James believed competition brings out the best in players and teams. In the following excerpt from a Thursday speech before the No. 6-ranked Huskies played at Arizona State, James discusses how UW defensive back Wayne Moses had caught UCLA running back James Owens, a sprinter, from behind in a game. On its face, the feat was impossible as Owens was faster than Moses. However, James said he had witnessed this phenomenon many times in his career—situations where athletes in the heat of competition somehow summon extraordinary strength or speed. He called it "putting on mental weight."

> We need to take this time to lift ourselves. Books are filled with Herculean performances of people—180-pounders whipping 220-pounders. We need to take our mental preparation and get faster than ever. Why do you hit harder in some games and get tougher than ever? Mentally you gear yourself to knock people back. You get bigger and stronger and take your opponent and whip him—regardless of size. How does this happen? We want to, in the Final 48 Hours, use quality time, additional film study, absolutely know all of your opponents' moves. Men this is a big game—our biggest yet! The chips are piling up—ASU has a lot in there. Get this one and it then gives us two weeks to improve as a team for our conference race.
>
> WINNING DYNAMICS. We have picked for emphasis to date: Aggression. Mental Toughness. Improve. Drive. I think everyone would agree that these four thoughts are particularly important for this game!! I mentioned last week that we were not close to our potential. Last Saturday—we got closer. An appropriate addition now is confidence under this category the trait emotional maturity.
>
> What is emotional maturity? It allows us to control emotions during competition. It allows us to convert anxiety or game tension so it is productive not destructive. It allows us to be calm and to think clearly in critical situations. Emotional maturity gives us poise, allows our emotions to help performance, not interfere with it. This trait, emotional maturity, has no respect for age or class. A freshman could have it. A senior could not. At times we have panicked when things have gone wrong. We did not versus Oregon. We did against Fresno State. We did not against Oregon State. This is the type of game—emotional—that will require being calm and thinking clearly in critical situations.

ASU. All I've heard from Tempe for one year is how they are out to get us. I heard it also about Wyoming—Utah—Oregon. My general thoughts are that they will be emotional. They will be jumping around excited—big crowd, lot of noise. But then we kick the damn thing off, it will be one of their guys out there against one of ours. The crowd will not play! (Coach Frank) Kush will not play! I look for blitzes by their defense. I look for rushes on our kicking game. I look for traps—toss sweeps. In other words, I expect their best shot.

Then I look for our emotional maturity. I look for you to be smart enough to know that this thing will last for 60 minutes. Just like the prizefight, the body punches, we're going after their ass for 60 minutes. We're going to pound them down. Wear them out. Hit! Hit! Hit! Then, in the third or fourth quarter, we're going to be able to name our score. We are going to Arizona for but one reason and don't forget it!!!!! Kick their ass.

The Sun Devils won this battle in the desert 12-7 as their defense shut down the Husky running game and ASU defensive end Bob Kohrs recovered a fumble for a touchdown. Coach Frank Kush announced three hours before the game that he had been fired because of allegations that he had punched a former ASU player during the 1978 Washington-ASU game. Kush was carried off the field by ASU players.

'You Don't Beat the Trojans with Finesse'
November 13, 1980

In his Thursday speech, before the 7-2 Huskies flew to Los Angeles to battle the nation's No. 2-ranked USC Trojans, James said he is motivated by his dreams. The Huskies, he said, could make a dream come true by snapping USC's 28-game unbeaten streak—the longest in the nation and in USC history.

James called USC one of the few iconic American sports teams that remains "eternally competitive." By whipping the Trojans, he said, the

Huskies could prove to the nation that Washington can build a team that commands respect like the best American sports teams ever. At this point in the season, the Huskies were 4-1 in conference play; the Trojans were undefeated in league play with one tie (4-0-1).

USC

The Trojans' unbeaten streak is at 28, longest in the nation and longest in school history. UW has not defeated USC in Los Angeles since 1964. Since we have been at UW, the Huskies are 2-3 versus the Trojans. In 1977, we generated six turnovers plus two blocked punts and won. In 1979, there were six fumbles, we got one, and lost a close game. It's important to make our own breaks.

Offense is averaging 27 points a game. Marcus Allen is No. 1 in league scoring with 13 touchdowns, No. 1 in league rushing with 154 yards a game, and second in the nation. Team is second in the league with 401.6 yards a game and first in rushing with 240.3 yards a game. They are eighth in passing yards with 161 yards on 21.7 attempts per game. WE MUST KEEP THIS GROUP OFF THE SCOREBOARD.

DEFENSE: This is their strength—this is why they're undefeated, allowing only 11.3 points per game. They are giving up 85 yards a game vs. the run for the last two opponents. Cal and Stanford had minus rushing yards against them. They are second in pass defense with 151 yards a game. Smith and Lott—safeties, fine athletes. Rangy linebackers, 6-foot-3, 6-4 and 6-5. Coach Robinson calls it his fastest defense ever. And it may be their best.

After describing the kicking match-ups, James declares: "We must win the kicking game" before settling into his general comments.

Game Thoughts. Team Image: USC. People—fans—coaches think what a team!! Big, strong, fast athletes—they have earned a special kind of respect. It's almost disbelief. "You really play for USC?" they ask. The Huskies are getting close to that. I too have goals—I draw my motivation from my dreams just as you do. I would like to prove to the sports fans and even those in academics that we can build a team that commands respect and deserves that kind of respect. I would like to show people that it can be done within the framework of the NCAA rules. By winning consistently you get it, by being eternally competitive.

Alabama—U.S.C. —they have it! So do the Yankees in baseball. The Boston Celtics in basketball had it! The Pittsburgh Steelers in pro football have it! In order to get that nationwide (worldwide) respect you have to do it more than once. The big one-time deal and you are considered Cinderella. She had the big one night out in her life. We don't want that. We want it year-in and year-out, week-in and week-out. You get it by winning big games. Beat one of those teams when it counts—USC—Yankees. Get to Pasadena again. Do it the right way by earning it outright. The '77 team did it, the '79 team beat Texas (in the Sun Bowl). Now the '80 team has an opportunity to cement the Husky image. We have to determine, each one of us, that they do have something that we want. We have to understand why they have the image. We then must realize what it will take. I think that on the first point that if I polled this squad that your determination would be evident.

Secondly, SC has their winning reputation—they have earned it on the field—they have a win streak going now. They have talent. They have reached a maturity level in their competition where they know they will get every opponent's best shot. The mature teams are seldom upset. Tough to defeat those teams—they have won many times on the last drive, the last shot, or the bottom of the ninth inning. We know what we want, a championship outright, BEAT USC's ASS.

Before big games in the past I've mentioned that they are won by people who want to win them the most. We were taught a couple of early lessons how to compete. Oregon and Navy certainly wanted to win more than us. Conversely, we taught Stanford, ASU, and Arizona a thing about winning big games.

We have found out some things about ourselves as a team: We discovered what we suspected all along—we can become a damn good team. We learned how to hit—how to play with reckless abandon, how enthusiasm and emotion could help us. We are on the verge of becoming an outstanding team! You become one when you defeat one. You are close to becoming a team that can go head-to-head with any team in the country. With two more solid outings and then six more weeks to point to the most visible college game of the year that is played Jan. 1 in Pasadena: You will be that team.

Then with three bowl teams in the past four seasons, you men will then have been a part in building the tradition and respect for yourself and Husky football that will soon be considered a program of excellence in college sports. It's not going to be an easy task but it will be well worth the effort. The USC defense admitted that they wanted to intimidate Stanford.

You don't beat the Trojans with finesse. You hit their ass. It's going to be a damn war and you had better prepare yourself for one. (USC Coach John) Robinson is talking National Championship. Let's end those dreams. Prepare yourself for a physical contest. There are a few things riding on this game—lots of chips, most are ours. We have got to go in knowing and believing you can get it done.

The No. 20-ranked Huskies, 11-point underdogs, believed—beating USC 20-10 as the defense forced eight turnovers. The Huskies clinched the Pac-10 Conference crown and a Rose Bowl berth. Ray Horton returned a punt 73 yards for a touchdown to spark the win.

'Net Genius at Work, Not Madman'
September 17, 1981

In his Thursday speech before the No. 15-ranked Huskies hosted Kansas State, James calls tennis star John McEnroe a great competitor. He references a column about McEnroe written by Steve Rudman, sportswriter for *The Seattle Post-Intelligencer* newspaper.

John McEnroe is the world's No. 1 tennis player. Steve Rudman's column in *The Seattle Post-Intelligencer* is titled, "Net Genius at Work, Not Madman."

James read a quote from McEnroe in the column:

> "You must develop a maniacal desire to win. For me this means expressing it in everything I do. I want my opponent to know how bad I want to win."

Then James paraphrases part of the column:

> Perfect: All McEnroe wants to do is be perfect, perfect on every point. That he can't—sometimes gives him fits. …. Once McEnroe, playing Tom Gullickson in an L.A. tourney. Fights for points. Match all but history—leading 6-2, 4-1, 30-love. Gullickson won a point—McEnroe slammed his racquet to the ground. It was an unimportant point to everyone but McEnroe. He detested losing it! Which is why he is tough to beat. He fights his guts out for every point. Even unimportant ones. That partially accounts for his success.

James then reviews the six characteristics of motivated people (from the Husky Playbook) and offers comments below each one.

1. Are Self-Starters
Drugs, alcohol, sleeping in. In one more week you're on your own—we move out of the fall camp concept. You've got to get yourself going—class—study—rest. Most of life failures can be related to these issues, people don't get up and get their day

started. People who are lazy sleep in. You must organize—budget your time.

2. Accept Responsibility

We, you, all of us, have responsibilities—team, family, school. Recognize it! We all want to go through life being responsible. We don't ever want to let people down. As a coach my job is to get you ready to play. There's a saying: "Do the thing you have to do better than you have to do it!" Accept leadership roles. Build a desire to take on more responsibility—get all you can!

3. Never Pass the Buck

When a mistake is made, accept responsibility. Don't alibi or blame others. Don't expect others to do what we must.

4. Look for Solutions, Not Excuses

People now expect us to win—they don't want to hear any excuses. The old saying is true in football: "Don't tell me about the pain, just show me the baby." We study history so we can eliminate mistakes. The past is over and we're going to play this season in the present.

5. Have Tremendous Drive and Energy

I have heard people say, "Why does he work so hard? Where does that guy get his drive? He's so enthusiastic!" Part of this is personality, drive, but basically it's tremendous drive! It's desire to be the best—to excel. Conditioning plays the greatest part! Lombardi's famous quote, "Fatigue makes cowards of us all" is true. Up 'til now, we have controlled your rest and diet. Now, for the rest of the season, you take on that responsibility. We will control rest and diet in the last 24 hours before the game. Diet—rest—and conditioning. It's difficult to have tremendous drive and energy if we don't do the above. Also, if we don't, we're more susceptible to injury and illness.

6. Move Forward with Dignity and Class.

We play the game honestly—fairly—and by rules. We don't want to be a talking team. We want to be a doing team—a team of action—let our opponents know how badly we want to win. We knock their asses off and pick them up. Never taunt. Class equals winner. We want to have just as much class off the field as on. All of the above equals winner!

Final Reminders: We are supposed to be the favorites—the better team! Kansas State has easily enough talent to win but ONLY IF our Final 48 Hours are not productive!!

In a game riddled with errors, the Huskies beat Kansas State 20-3. Sophomore quarterback Steve Pelluer threw a 69-yard touchdown strike to Anthony Allen early in the final quarter to put the game out of reach. Each team committed five turnovers.

Eight Points of Being a Better Competitor
September 16, 1982

In his Thursday speech, before the No. 1-ranked Huskies played at Arizona in the season's second game, James articulated his "Eight Points of Being a Better Competitor." He then closed with a focus on "Championship Game No. 1" for the Huskies, who destroyed Texas-El Paso 55-0 in the season-opener.

Competing and Preparation

As I mentioned Monday, Arizona probably is the best team physically that we will face during these first seven weeks. Eight points that will make us better competitors:
   1) Have some fun.
   2) Keep our emotions on an even keel.
   3) Practice difficult techniques.
   4) Build your own confidence.
   5) Keep pouring it on.
   6) Consider difficult conditions an advantage.
   7) Make every play critical.
   8) Fresh mind on every play, every day.

This game is Championship Game No. 1. It's just as important as the last one. I'm tired of hearing how big a game it is for them. How they have pointed to it for so long. How much they have at stake. Bullshit—it's just as big or bigger for us. We have a hell of a lot at stake. As far as we're concerned it's the biggest game of the year.

We know who wins big games: The team that wants it the most. We're foolish as hell if we don't want it more than Arizona. If we don't try harder! Hit harder!

Linebacker Mark Stewart recovered two fumbles in the first half to set up Steve Pelluer touchdown passes of 10 and 16 yards to Willie Rosborough and Paul Skansi, respectively, as the Huskies coasted to a 20-0 halftime lead and a 23-13 win over the Wildcats.

Battles Must Be Won to Get a Chance to Win War
November 8, 1984

In his Thursday speech before the 9-0 and No. 1-ranked Huskies traveled to Los Angeles to play No. 14 USC in their most important game of the year to date, James opened his comments saying battles must be won to have a chance to win the war. Beating the Trojans would give the Huskies a chance to win the war, namely the Pac-10 Conference crown and national championship.

A lot of this is history but it's important that we win the major portion of these battles. Again, identify your role for this game and your contribution. You must win.

After comparing the teams' strengths on offense, defense, and kicking game, James speaks of the paramount role of mental preparation.

Now the mental part. How do WE treat this the championship game? We draw on our experiences—nine games this year in 1984, plus 1983 and 1982, high school and all of our competitive lives provide experience for this game. We've put in a plan—you've practiced it. NOW we master it and build on every aspect of our mental, emotional, and physical performance. It will dictate: How we play! How we work! How we hit!

After reviewing the team's emphasis for each of the first nine games of the season, James closes:

Finally a look at our winning edge! Discipline—some football played by rules limit mistakes.

Conditioning—we're OK. Toughness—we must be the toughest Husky team ever. Kicking—going good, just eliminate two to three problems. We must win the kicking game!

Tailback Fred Crutcher rushed for 116 yards and a touchdown, and Frank Jordan kicked three field goals to lift USC to a 16-7 victory. Crutcher scored on a 2-yard run in the final period to bring the Trojans back from a 7-6 deficit.

Why Motivate?
September 19, 1985

In this Thursday speech before the Huskies traveled to play the University of Houston in the third game of the season, James shows how he approached leadership when things were going badly. James and his Huskies were being criticized in the media and by fans after starting the season ranked No. 12 in the nation before losing 31-17 to Oklahoma State, and 31-3 to Brigham Young. Here, James takes the emphasis off winning and asks that players simply focus on game-preparation. He reminds players that the Thursday speeches are designed to motivate them to prepare well so they will perform well. The Huskies, at this point, are desperately in need of some confidence and motivation.

Motivation. A reminder of the purpose of this meeting! I'm trying to motivate you. I'm trying to get you started on the mental preparation of this game ahead of our next opponents.

Most coaches have a meeting similar to this. Most have it on Friday. Ours is 48 hours before the game rather than 24 hours. But why? Why worry? Why motivate? My biggest job is to get maximum productivity out of each man in here—to get you to play harder, to get you to concentrate better, to get you mentally and physically tougher.

Some additional thoughts: Robert Schuller's book, I have talked to you about it before, *Tough Times Never Last, But Tough People Do!* So basically, if we are tough people and we want to turn this thing around, we will last. I haven't noticed anyone quitting. We're here to stay. Nothing ever stays the same. We get better or poorer—moving forward or backward, better physically, mentally, now it's mental (the Final 48 Hours). Don't want (anyone) feeling sorry for themselves. Tough people don't do that—they fight! They get their ass back up off the ground and compete. In our scouting report, "The price of success," read the last paragraph and every man should ask himself:

"Am I willing to endure the pain of this struggle for the comforts and rewards and the glory that go with achievement? Or, shall I accept the uneasy and inadequate contempt that comes with mediocrity?" Am I willing to pay the price of success? Am I willing to pay the price of success? Sometimes, no, most times, it will be an incredible price. That's why many don't buy it.

As I said in our first meeting, total commitment is required—submerge, not just up to the waist—all the way in competitively. Sure we have young players in many key roles! Many have to play more. In my press conferences, I've mentioned youth and injuries. I want you to know that I don't believe in excuses. I say these things before games to soften the opponent. Youth is not an excuse—many play successfully every day in all sports. You simply make up for your experience with better preparation! Better effort! Better concentration!

You should live with a projector and film. I've seen players fumble one week and get hit twice as hard the next game and the ball doesn't come out. We must protect the football at all costs. Tackling? Get yourself in proper position. Get yourself to the ball. Gang tackling teams don't let the runners get to the open field. We still can be a "good team" in '85. We improved this week. We still can be champions—there are nine days left before the conference race begins. Our emphasis must be on preparation, not on winning.

Final 48 Hours. If we prepare properly the winning will come. We've faced adversity: Injured players; defeats—we've suffered. We've been told suffering builds endurance—from the Bible! So much has been written about roadblocks, obstacles, adversity, winners turn them into positives. Let's turn it into a plus! When our team is defeated—it becomes more determined, and the loss helps us down the road. Injure a knee? Rehabilitate it and make it stronger. Injure an arm—build up the legs. Injure a leg—build up the arms. If a receiver injures a leg he can catch a thousand balls, and becomes a better receiver. If a starter is injured, the back-up gets valuable work and experience. When injuries affect running game, our passing game gets better! When injuries affect passing game, our running game gets better!

So, you see, the adversity we've faced can and will make us better if we approach this in the right way.

Remember failure will never overtake you if your determination to succeed is strong enough. Incidentally, the Bottom Ten poll, we are No. 1. That's the poll that selects the 10 poorest teams. We have been chosen as the worst team, two weeks of being No. 1 of the worst. We should be able to get some motivation from that—let's go to work.

Jeff Jaeger booted a school-record five field goals and fullback Rick Fenney scored on a 1-yard plunge to lift the Huskies to a 29-12 victory over Houston—ending their two-game losing skid. The Huskies won their next four games to salvage the 1985 season, finishing 7-5, including a win over Colorado in the Freedom Bowl. As James had urged them, the Huskies leveraged their adversity to become better.

'20 Questions'
September 15, 1988

In his Thursday speech before the 1-0 Huskies hosted Army, James offered a different approach to his motivational talk. He offered "20 Questions" to sharpen the Huskies' competitive edge:

> 20 Questions—used to be a TV show. You had 20 questions to determine the identity of the person, thing, etc. I believe there are 20 questions that we need to be asking ourselves. We have a primary concern—competition, the better it is the better you become. A lot of people believe this! They believe that you play to the level of the opponent. I don't believe this has to be true. Sure you have upsets. Playing our first six games we have two distinct levels of competition. We have three non-league teams that don't enjoy prestige image of the second three opponents. The first three are Purdue, Army, San Jose State, and our second three are UCLA, ASU, and USC.
>
> So the real key question is: How do we defeat the second group if we play to the level of the first? These, then, are the questions that have to be answered correctly in order for this team to reach our goals. So, if we can get the right answers to these 20 questions, we will be ready!!
>
> 1. How am I progressing as a team player! Go back and read in your playbook the Five Major Ingredients to Squad Development.
> 2. Have I given 100 percent? Judge yourself—70—80—90—100 percent?
> 3. Have I shown courage? On and off the field!

4. Have I learned what to do? Know your position!

5. Have I put team goals first?

6. Have I been loyal to my teammates and coaches?

7. Can I discipline myself to take care of all of my team requirements? Especially when school starts? Meetings, classes, weights, study table, treatment.

8. Am I willing to obey training rules this fall so I can be at my best—tobacco, alcohol, drugs?

9. Will I play as hard and be alert vs. Army as UCLA?

10. Will I prepare as well for Army as for USC?

11. Will I get my game face on and "mentally get totally into the game" the same for Army as for ASU, UCLA, and USC?

12. Do I really want this to be a great fall? Freshmen, sophomores, juniors, seniors, redshirts? The seniors are running out of time and we need everyone!

13. Could I play for an NFL team based on the way I played last Saturday and will play this week?

14. Am I willing to pay the price to get myself ready to play this week? Will I pay the price? Will I perform my visualization work in the Final 48 Hours and use my time well to energize?

15. Do I really know my opponent? Don't just see the film one or two times. Memorize it! Live with it!

16. Do I know my plan and can I make it work against new things they show? We were picked as their biggest game outside of rivalries for 1988. Don't you know they will have new things for us!

17. Will I let them fool me? Fake field-goal, fake punt, reverse, all-out rush! Stay alert mentally!

18. Will I hit for 60 minutes? How tough will we be?

19. Will I attempt to hit harder this week than I ever have in my career? Be more aggressive!

20. Will I ever get a personal record each game this fall? That's being a better player with each game experience!

Men, this all starts with Saturday. We answer to ourselves and to our teammates. One game at a time. On Saturday at 1 p.m., on the Astroturf, Army is up! We are pointing to Oct. 1 (vs. UCLA) and Nov. 19 (last game of the year vs. WSU). We take care of Army and we will be ready when those dates arrive!

Vince Weathersby ran for two touchdowns and Chico Fraley returned a pass interception 72 yards for the final score with 1:10 left to power the Huskies past the pesky Cadets 31-17.

A 'Team-Building Exercise'
September 14, 1989

In his Thursday speech before the 1-0 and No. 15-ranked Huskies hosted Purdue, James introduced a "team-building exercise."

Additional Thoughts. We want an edge, and we get that through practice, talent, and preparation. This is called a team-building exercise. I'll ask questions, give you a moment to answer! Think about them, come up with ideas, and mention them to your coaches.

1. What did I do to help us work well together as a team last week?

2. What did my teammates do that helped us work well together as a team?

3. What were the things that we did last week in a big game that helped us work well together?

4. What do we need to improve as a team and to be more successful?

5. What can I do personally to encourage and support my teammates?

New Team Affirmations: Affirmations for Being a Team Player! We set goals and we set affirmations that would help us stay focused in order to reach those goals. To continue to grow into a great team or a championship team, we must improve as team players. All of us! Coaches too. We have already five ingredients for squad development!! Hustle 100 percent, have courage, learn assignments, care about winning, and be loyal. Now let me list some team affirmations for being a team player—individuals either tear down or build up a team!

- I enjoy encouraging and supporting my teammates!
- I am a good team player.
- I assist and help my teammates in any way I can.
- When my teammate wins, I win!
- I believe in myself and my teammates!
- I believe I can count on my teammates!
- We work together well as a team!
- We have fun playing together!
- We are proud of our team!
- We play with intensity and focus!
- The pride is back. We earned respect and plan to keep it!

Now, let's bring it to the present tense. How do teams react after a big win? Everyone knows teams don't remain the same—they get better or get poorer. Poor-Thinking Teams. They lack competitive maturity, and believe what they hear and read. Friends, media all say "you guys are great!" They think they have arrived, "we've done all that we have to do!" They forget immediately what it took to get there: All the weights, all the physical work, and all the mental work. They don't give lesser opponents the respect they deserve. They don't prepare in the future like they did prior to a big game. They start to get an inflated opinion of themselves, a "big head." It's party time, celebration time for them. They set themselves up to be upset!

Winners, Champions. They add the one key ingredient that poor-thinking teams lacked: confidence as a team! They start believing good things would happen, rather that just hoping they would. They increase their effort, and find that their concentration and focus improve. They train better—and realize they have more to gain from it! They start believing more in themselves and teammates. They block for runners and passers! They rush hard, coverage is there! They know that things don't get easier—that people will come after us harder as winners.

Champions have that maturity as a team. They Win! They Win! It's great! But it only gets tougher, never easier!

Question: Do you think Miami got Purdue's best shot? Do you think we will? You bet we will! Our goal is to become even better team players: Out-prepare Purdue. Out-hit Purdue. Out-hustle Purdue.

Heeding James' words, the Huskies raised their competitiveness, clobbering Purdue 38-9—their ninth win in a row over a Big Ten Conference opponent. Washington also recorded its two longest non-scoring plays in its 100-year football history to date—a 78-yard run by Grew Lewis and a 76-yard pass from Cary Conklin to Andre Riley.

A Turning Point in Huskies' Competitiveness
September 20, 1990

In his Thursday speech before taking on three-time Pac-10 Champion and No. 5-ranked USC, which had defeated Washington the previous four consecutive years, James challenged the Huskies to achieve true competitive greatness. The Huskies had narrowly won their first two games of the season over inferior opponents, beating San Jose State 20-17 and Purdue 20-14.

Following his review of the Pyramid of Objectives, and the Trojans' strengths, James launched one of his most effective motivational talks ever regarding competitive greatness—a speech that can be said to have begun the Huskies' march to the national championship the following season.

Additional Comments, Focus on Challenge at Hand! A few comments about our first two games! We played two decent teams and obviously won. We played to each other's level—the statistics were close. Take past records out—league image, school names and you've got teams that appeared even. In our first two games against San Jose State and Purdue you have three teams that appeared even. Either team could have easily won both games on one play! But you can't convince me that either team is as talented as us.

Let's talk for a moment about another team. The U.S. Olympic Hockey Team 1980! We matched up very well with every country but Canada and Russia! We had college athletes on the U.S. Team vs. national teams! Kids vs. veterans. Russia was a team that not only defeated National Hockey League teams in exhibition, Russia defeated a team of NHL All Stars. They (the U.S. and Russia) met for the gold medal at Lake Placid, N.Y., in the winter of 1980. U.S. Coach Herb Brooks frankly told his players "gentlemen, you don't have enough talent to win on talent alone." With those words ringing in their ears, they pulled off the greatest upset in Olympic History!!

Each individual clearly needed something beyond himself to overcome a great team. Yet, without a powerful Russian team opposing them, they could never have risen to such heights! The challenge of the Russians was needed to transform the Americans into all they could become. We are in a somewhat similar situation. We could continue to play the San Jose States and the Purdues of college football, win some games, have a good record. However, it will take a USC, Colorado (whom the Huskies face the following week) to bring us up to another level of competition—a level much higher than that at which we have been playing! A level, I believe, we are capable of getting to.

What was the benefit of our first two games? We had to fight to win both games—60 minutes, playing under pressure. We were playing on the road and on grass at Purdue. We were playing as favorites and saw firsthand how underdogs compete. Teams will mark their calendar and point to us. They respect your name, your tradition. All games will be tough unless injuries alter things. All of our remaining opponents should be better than San Jose State and Purdue. So we needed to struggle the first two games. We needed the full 60 minutes and the pressure. We needed to get new starters game experience. Now, we need USC to get us to another playing level!

Why USC? They're good! They have defeated us four straight years—payback. There's not a player in here with a win over USC! They are the three-time Pac-10 champions. They are the Rose Bowl champions. They are ranked in the Top 10 in the nation, undefeated. The key thing is we need to get to a higher level!! Also, we need a top opponent, the atmosphere of a big game, TV. We also need to get the conference pride back up north. Also we need to know USC will be out of the race, three years is enough. Also we need to bring humility back to their program. Also we need to take away some S.C. arrogance. Also we need the confidence gained from this "big win." Stated simply, we need a big victory!

On top of all your preparation this week, we need to set a couple of attitudes to get this job done! First, we need an attitude of how important this game is! We need an attitude of they are good and this will be a tough-assed, hard-nosed game! We need an attitude of Game Face—no bullshit, let's get it on! The attitude of there's not many days in our lives quite like this one. An attitude of save nothing, leave my guts out on that field. Like Nike says, "Just Do It!" Let's get to work!

The No. 21-ranked Huskies took James' words to heart. Greg Lewis rushed for 126 yards, Eric Briscoe picked off two passes, and sophomore quarterback Mark Brunell outplayed Todd Marinovich to lead a 31-0 rout. It was the Trojans' first shutout loss since Arizona State beat them 28-0 in 1985. In his third start for the Huskies, Brunell completed 12 of 23 passes for 197 yards and one touchdown, and ran for 38 yards on eight carries. The Huskies, who lost at Colorado 20-14 the following week, finished the season 10-2 and beat Iowa 46-34 in the Rose Bowl. In many ways, however, it was this dominating win that would set the stage for their ascension to the national championship the following season.

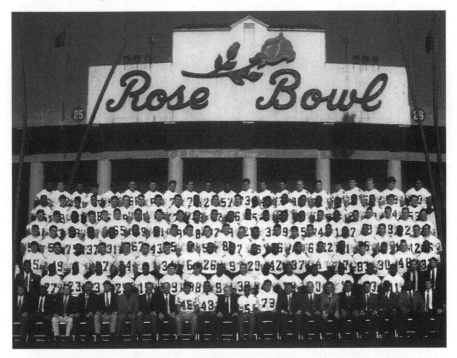

The University of Washington 1991 National Championship team went 12-0 and beat Michigan in the Rose Bowl.   *UW Photo*

Hoist the Black Flag, and Begin Slitting Throats
October 4, 1990

In his Thursday speech after the 3-1 Huskies narrowly lost at Colorado and before they traveled to play Arizona State, James emphasized the importance of the mental and emotional aspects of football. Once again, he pushed competitive greatness and urged the No. 17-ranked

Huskies to become "consistently competitive." Citing Olympic gymnast Nadia Comaneci from Romania as an example of a mature competitor, James enlivens his speech with quotes from several famous folks, including writer H. L. Mencken.

> Let's talk more on the mental and emotional aspects of the game! Why it all boils down to competitive performance! We're seeking to become a consistently competitive team! It takes maturity as competitors—it's immature to ever think a win will be automatic. Mature competitors don't have letdowns! They don't have bad days! Mature competitors say "When it counts, I'm always there." Again, championship teams get this done. We must have our best day on game day. Each game day we must be better! We're always good daily but always at our best on game day. That's maturity. Then on big game days we give a little bit more!

> Nadia Comaneci, a 14-year-old Romanian gymnast, was expected to be a tough competitor in the 1976 Olympics. No one expected her to perfect! Yet the judges could find no flaws in her balance beam routine and she was awarded the first perfect 10 in Olympic history! She wasn't through. She stunned the world with seven perfect scores and won three gold medals— for the uneven bars, balance beam and individual all-around. She reached a competitive performance of "best in world" champion and stayed there for years.

> We are asking for best in Pac-10. We are asking for seven games! We are asking for no letdowns, no bad days, just consistent championship performance. You have talent! You have developed it! Now, perform to it! We need execution on game day. Take advantage of opportunities. You get execution on game day by getting execution on weekdays, Monday, Tuesday, Wednesday, Thursday, Friday.

> There are basically 28 more practice opportunities! You see, everyone needs insurance in life. This is our insurance in

football. We take care of the Huskies, the Huskies will handle these next opponents. The price? Rest, nutrition, practice, weight training, mental preparation. We let up in any one area and we've lost our insurance. Nadia reached perfection. We're searching for Nadia's perfection!

A quote from author H. L. Mencken talks about crisis times in our lives, whether war or personally being attacked. There are parallels in sports. (Quoting Mencken) "Every normal man must be tempted, at times, to spit on his hands, hoist the black flag, and begin slitting throats." Obviously, we can't go slitting throats but we can hoist our personal black flag. This is our war. Arizona State is in our way. We talked last week about 60 tough SOBs getting on the bus. That game in Boulder (at University of Colorado where the Huskies lost 20-14) last week was a battle, a street fight. Controlled by rules but it was a tough, hard-nosed, two-fisted football game. No place for cowards!

Quote from Sam Huff, great New York Giants linebacker: "People pay money to see great hits!" Quote from Howie Long, Oakland Raiders: "They call me caveman because of the way I attack people. I like to think of myself as relentless." Quote from *Chariots of Fire* (the movie): "Let each of you discover where your chance for greatness lies. Seize that chance and let no power on earth deter you." Well, this can be a great team. We have our chance, it may be our only chance! Think of yourself as relentless, attack your man! Give the people what they pay to see: great hits! Give yourself what you have worked for! Give yourself what you are capable of! Give Arizona State a shit-kicking! ASU preparation takes priority in our lives for the next 48 hours!

The Huskies responded, beating Arizona State 42-14 as Greg Lewis rushed for 159 yards and three touchdowns, and Beno Bryant returned a punt 82 yards for another score.

'You Shouldn't Taunt the Huskies'
November 1, 1990

In this Thursday speech before the 7-1 and No. 7-ranked Huskies (5-0 in league play) hosted Arizona after crushing California 46-7 the previous week, James reminded the team of where it was a mere six weeks ago. At that time, James urged the Huskies to rise to a higher level of competitiveness after unremarkable wins over San Jose State and Purdue to open the season. Six weeks prior, James had challenged the Huskies to live up to their potential, and they did—devastating USC 31-0. Again beating the drum of competitive greatness, James underscores what the Huskies have accomplished and anticipates what lies ahead.

> Championship Game No. 6. How far you have come in such a short period of time. Six weeks ago today, we were preparing for USC. We talked about our struggles vs. San Jose State and Purdue in the first two games of this season. We knew we had to get to another level vs. USC and Colorado. That challenge was what we needed at that point in time. If we had continued to play average teams, we may have continued to play at their level. But we knew we were facing a moment of truth. You have met every challenge! You have gotten better daily, which also means weekly!
>
> However, you have not gotten the respect—there were doubters always. "No way you will stay up! No way you will stay focused!" From ESPN, CNN, ABC, you couldn't compete three weeks in a row? We heard it from opposing coaches. From opposing players. Even last week our own paper, the *Seattle P-I* picked Cal. And now, lo and behold, we get it from Arizona players, the press and their coach. This is fine, freedom of speech, people can say what they want. But men, when they do this, two things occur: 1. They question us as competitors. They are saying that we are not that good. They are saying all teams have letdowns so the 1990 Huskies will

also. 2. The second thing that occurs is they are indicting us as competitors and our ability to play out an 11-game schedule.

Well, every team doesn't do this let-up. Great teams have one consistent characteristic. No matter who they play. They just play hard, get better, they win! I thought we might totally be finished with the doubters. I guess not. I thought by now our opponents, players, and coaches, might have learned a lesson. Talk is cheap—save your energy for game time. You shouldn't taunt the Huskies. You shouldn't ever question our desire to compete!

Last Saturday after the California game (which the Huskies won 46-7), I told you that there was one game on this year's schedule that I put a mark by. I know there are 17 days 'til WSU and 61 days 'til the Rose Bowl. But my motivation was directed to Nov. 3, our game against Arizona in two days. Since 1987, I've been frustrated with Arizona—the ties, the defeats, the way we played, and with their arrogance! So Championship Game No. 6 is here. This is the biggest one of all. We can end it all right here on Saturday. We can end the championship race and years of frustration.

Can you believe the quote by their beat writer Corky Simpson, "The truth is Arizona presents a lot more problems for Washington than vice-versa. You have to catch them first though, and against Arizona that is a special problem. Give Michael Bates a half-step and try to catch him—see how far Lamont Lovett can run through a sliver of daylight—try to arm-tackle Mike Striednig or Mario Hampton and they'll put hoof prints on your chest. Play the pitch too eagerly against Ronald Veal and watch his dust, etc."

A few weeks ago I told you about our 1980 U.S. Hockey Gold Medal Team. I told you what Coach Herb Brooks told his team as they started to prepare: "Men you don't have the talent to win on talent alone." He knew they would be underdogs, would have to train, would have to get stronger, would have to practice like hell, and would have to come together as a team. Well, on the day of the final game with Russia he told them a few other things: "You're born to be a player. You're meant to be here. You're meant to be here at this time. The moment is ours!"

I'm feeling the same way: We have had quite a challenge. We still have a big job ahead of us. We still have our doubters. Let's silence the critics. Let's put an end to that statement that UW hasn't defeated Arizona since 1984. Let's kick their ass! I believe this moment is ours! Want to ensure victory? Six weeks ago, we got to another level of performance. Well, let's turn it up another notch! Let's just see how good this team of ours can become!

The Huskies demolished Arizona, 54-10, and clinched their first Rose Bowl trip in nine years. Mark Brunell passed for two touchdowns and ran for a third, while Greg Lewis rushed for 103 yards on 22 carries, including a 5-yard touchdown run. It was the 14th 100-yard rushing game for Lewis.

'The Race Now Is for the National Title'
November 8, 1990

In his Thursday speech after steamrolling Arizona and before hosting UCLA, James told the 8-1 and Rose Bowl-bound Huskies (6-0 in league play) that the "race now is for the national title." The Huskies were ranked No. 2 in the nation at the time.

James' review of the year's objectives shows just how dominating the 1990 Huskies had been—beating opponents by an average of 31.8 points per game (beating Arizona by 44, California by 37 and Stanford by 36) since their only loss, 20-14 at Colorado, in the fourth game of the season.

James shares the statistical highlights of the Huskies' reign of terror thus far in 1990:

You have worked your butts off to get these numbers, let's keep it up—this is also the reason for lopsided scores! No. 1 in total offense at 422.3 yards per game this season. No. 1 in total defense at 278.1 yards per game. No. 1 in scoring offense, 35.2 points per game. No. 1 in scoring defense, holding opponents to 12.8 points per game. No. 1 in punt returns with 15.9 yards per return. No. 1 in turnovers with +17. No. 1 in fourth-quarter points, +46. No. 1 in rushing defense, 65.7 yards per game. No. 1 in pass defense efficiency. No. 1 in first downs allowed. No. 1 in allowing third-down conversions on defense, 26.5 percent. No. 1 in quarterback sacks with 40 for minus 309 yards. No. 1 in fewest quarterback sacks allowed, 14.

The race now is for the national title. We will use the same approach that has worked so well. We need to take care of UCLA. That's all we can do. That's all we need to do. The Pac-10 Championship is won. However, we don't want it shaded. We are guaranteed at least (8-3). We could be (9-2). But 10-1 is the record we must carry to Jan. 1.

What This Game Means to Us? Motivation? Obviously, a win means we will stay in the race for No. 1 in the nation. A win means a California sweep—a Sunbelt sweep—for us and our seniors. I don't have to say much. This is an incredible oppor-tunity. Let's look at these one at a time. California sweep. They are the so-called "gifted schools." Northwest schools are looked at as second-class citizens. For many years there has been talk about breaking up the league—throw the Northwest schools out (except UW). Well, we can sweep these gifted higher education institutions. Glamour schools! In 1977, we defeated all four but one was by forfeit. 1964 was the last time UW defeated all four on the field of play—26 years. Sun Belt Sweep. We can beat all six Sun Belt schools in the Pac-10 in one season. It's never been done! That would be quite an achievement!

Let's now consider the seniors. This will be the last time our seniors will play before a home crowd in our own stadium—ever. Some might think, "So what. What's the big deal?" I'll tell you why it's a big deal. I've been there many times. I've seen senior classes do it here! Sixteen now. The guys will always remember this game. That's why it is so important! Think of the trips down the tunnel to go to practice. Think of the home games of their career—four years (24) five years (30). Remember the great victories—bitter defeats! The great post-game celebrations. It's hard to capture anything like it the rest of your life. Great joys. Events the rest of your life will be in much smaller groups with family, friends. Yes and remember the impact the bad times had on your lives. Bitter disappointments. These guys all lived through the 6-5 season of 1988 even the victories were labeled ugly. We even suffered after the six victories. We could never satisfy our fans, the press, yes, even ourselves. That was the first team to NOT get a bowl bid in 10 years here.

These are also the guys who were part of a rebirth of determination around here to see that this didn't happen again—this senior class and last year's! Well, these seniors have paid an incredible price to get us back! Think for a moment of the time spent in the weight room—this is the strongest Husky football team ever! Don't forget the "winter mat program"—guys throwing up—busting their butts—this is the quickest, hardest-working team in 16 years. The speed classes and the remarkable improvement in our 40-yard dash times. This team has to also be the fastest in Husky history. Don't also forget the trips to the training room for treatment of bumps, bruises, sprains, and illness. And in some cases trips to the hospital for surgery: two knees, one back, two shoulder surgeries from this group. So what do we owe the seniors? Something they will not forget. Simply put, a victory. A great home victory—a team PR (personal record) our very best! A victory that could possibly move us to No. 1.

One last point for you returning players: Next time you play UCLA is Oct. 16, 1993. They are off the schedule until then. Give them something to remember us for! Hoist the black flag one more time, at home the last time, for these seniors!

Brad Daluiso's 43-yard field goal with 10 seconds left on the clock lifted UCLA to a 25-22 victory in the wind and rain at Husky Stadium. The Huskies had tied the score (22-22) with 2:36 remaining on a 32-yard pass from Mark Brunell to Mario Bailey and Brunell's 2-point conversion. Washington's hopes for a national championship would be postponed.

VISUALIZING VICTORY

Introduction

As I've noted, James urged players to use the final 48 hours before kickoff to visualize themselves winning their own individual battles and the game. James believed strongly in the power of visualization in the final 48 hours to improve the Huskies, individually and as a team. He studied visualization and the psychological aspects involved throughout his career and grew thoroughly convinced it gave the Huskies a win-ning edge. A significant and growing body of research supports the effectiveness of visualization. The Thursday speeches show how James' instructions to players became increasingly specific as his knowledge of performance-enhancing visualization increased, and as it evolved to help the players. James expected his players to not only prepare well mentally for games but to actually use their mental visualization work to improve as players in the final 48 hours.

Preparing to Ground Air Force
September 11, 1980

In the following portion of a Thursday speech before the No. 19-ranked Huskies prepared to host 2-0 Air Force Academy, James notes specifically what he expects from players in the final 48 hours. Also, he suggests that the national championship is within their reach.

> Let's Talk About Us and Getting Ready to Compete! I like to take this first game each year and talk about getting ready to play, getting up! Getting psyched! On game day, many strange things can and have happened. Good and bad performances! Big wins, big upsets! Most coaches talk to players and the team about improving when you're not on the field practicing. They talk about improving when the fall season's over—when winter weights and conditioning starts up. They talk about improving when spring ball's over: summer weights and workouts. We talk about improving 48 hours prior to kick-off. Some teams use these 48 hours to get great mental preparation. Some play-ers do and some don't; when they don't, you don't get good team victories. Sometimes you get defeats—just like a car doesn't run well on only half of its cylinders. So our goal today is to arm ourselves with ideas that will do one thing: Prepare ourselves to achieve—get our best performance.

> So 67 hours from Wednesday evening's practice until kickoff, we work 80 minutes. The rest is mental and rest. We must:

1. Respect opponent.

2. Use quiet time to think and concentrate.

3. We want to play good this week and then get better each week. No peaks, no valleys—consistent steady performance.

4. What you would like from mental preparation is that it makes you better. Your best performance should come on game day. Some athletes break records only in practice. Champions get their outstanding performance in competition. You've all competed, you should know what works best. If your performance doesn't improve appreciably you need to work on these important two days. Want to play better than ever, each time out? Then Prepare Better!!!

Let's Examine First Errors that Some Make in Game Preparation:

1. Wait until kickoff or first hit, then get fired up.

2. Expect your coaches to fire you up. Pep talk.

3. Some worry themselves sick.

4. Some see only negative thoughts—question their ability.

5. Some think they can get up by watching TV.

6. Some think they can get up by listening to radios. Entertainment can relax an individual, take your mind off the game, but it doesn't improve performance.

How Do Successful Athletes and Coaches (Competitors) Prepare? First rule—need quality quiet time for productivity. Alert—at meetings hear, learn, question, concentrate. Film study: Respect opponent No. 1, know opponent No. 2. Quiet time—play the game in your mind—assignments, etc. Use of senses sight—sound—smell—feel. Control groups psychologists have proven one group practices physically, another mentally. The performance results are close. Some record messages on tapes and play over and over. Great athletes get their game face on early and want to be alone in the final 24 hours. They want no idle conversations, they want to concentrate.

Review. We want to use the Final 48 Hours to be productive. We don't want to peak on Thursday and go down by Saturday. We want to be better on Game Day. Use Thursday and Friday to get bigger, stronger, faster and quicker. We don't want to bother one other person in their approach. Don't entertain—keep quiet—no radios on trip. Mental preparation is like religion: each man in his own way. Then we play with great excitement. Then we play with enthusiasm. Then we play with great intensity

Remember the first game of the 1980 edition of Husky Football. New team personality, sure we have a tradition to uphold and we want to. We can also accomplish some things that have never been done here, go 12-0 and become NATIONAL CHAMPIONS.

One other thing: Air Force is 2-0 and is in our stadium. Let's put a finish to that bullshit now.

Tom Flick completed 18 of 24 passes for 316 yards, including an 84-yard scoring pass to Willie Rosborough on the third offensive play of the game, as the Huskies clobbered Air Force, 50-7. Tailback Toussaint Tyler scored on runs of 34, 3, and 1 yards while Kyle Stevens scored on runs of 21 and 7 yards.

The Final 48 Hours Must Improve Performance
November 3, 1988

In his Thursday speech as the struggling 5-3 Huskies prepared to host Arizona, James reminded players and coaches that the stakes remained high for the three games left in the regular season, including a possible bowl game. James focused on the importance of using the final 48 hours well.

Even though football is a team game, it's made up of key individual battles. On each play there are four to eight players near the point of attack. We have to get ourselves ready to win those key battles in kicking game, offense, and defense. We must do a better job of getting every man ready to play. You are responsible! For you. You are accountable! For you. You must light your own damn fire! Whatever your ritual was for your personal record in the past, you must repeat!

If we do, we will become mature competitors! Mature competitors compete like hell every play! They play every day! They don't wait until Saturday, "Coach I'll show them." That's bullshit. You compete like hell every day and you can go to sleep at night knowing you did your best.

When you leave this program, you can look back and honestly say "I became as good a player as I possibly could because I gave it my best and competed hard every day." It's the only way to reach your full potential. Anything less than that and you have let yourself and your teammates down! You see, playing three or four good games and three or four average games is an indictment on ourselves as competitors. Getting to the top is an incredibly difficult journey. Staying there is even tougher! You're there—Division 1-A major college football. The better you play this game the harder people come after you—as an individual! As a team!

I have seen it with this program. We are now everyone's big game. Think Arizona prepared for California like they will us? Hell no! Late in the season—real key games left around the league! A number of teams can go 7-4, 8-3. It's that time in the season for injuries and most everyone is bruised! Replacement players must respond and rise to the occasion! L.A. Dodgers were not supposed to win the division—they did. They were not supposed to beat the Mets—World Series, they did. Now in it (World Series) and they're not supposed to beat Oakland

A's, they did. Each game they were not supposed to win? And they did! How did they with replacements—back-ups, getting key players hurt each game? How did they win?

They thought they could when no one else did! They produced when given the opportunity! They had a pitcher named Bulldog who basically said, "let's just go play! Your best against mine." A special kind of mental toughness. Had a lot of injuries but the back-ups came in and made the plays. He wanted—dreamed of the chance—to play in a "big game." A couple players were discards who had to beg to get the chance to just be on the roster. We need a few Bulldogs.

So we recognize we need to put this team concept together. Good kicking. Good offense. Good defense. We get this by getting ready to play as individuals. There is a price to pay in everything—turn the TV and radios off, lock in on the game. We get this by individuals kicking the shit out of individuals that you go up against. We get this by lighting our fire. We get this by each individual on this team saying, "My one and only responsibility for the next 45 hours is to get me ready to play."

Doug Pfaff kicked a 22-yard field goal with 5 seconds left on the clock to lift Arizona to a 16-13 victory. The winning score was set up by a sack of quarterback Cary Conklin that resulted in an Arizona fumble recovery on the Washington 6-yard-line with 55 seconds remaining.

'Using the Final 48 Hours to Get Better'
September 7, 1989

In his Thursday speech before Washington hosted Texas A&M in the season-opener, James reminds the team of the purpose and function of the Thursday speeches. He does this before providing detailed instructions on how to best use the final 48 hours before kickoff to improve. The game presents an opportunity for the Huskies to avenge a 29-12 loss at Texas A&M in 1987.

Using the Final 48 Hours to Get Better

Fact—You can better physically by using mental process. Fact—
You can't continue to practice physically but you can run plays
through your minds 500 times or more before the game. Teams
that play the best are teams that think the most about the game.
Games that mean the most get more mental attention! Everyone
gets their game face on some time prior to kickoff. That means
the time that you can't get your mind off the game! Fact—the
earlier the better! If this is true, we should want to do this! How
do we go about this? Must be in a quiet setting. The hardest
thing is to stay focused and avoid interruptions.

Pick up the feel of the game day, smell the field, hear the
sounds in the stadium. You're not in the stands seeing yourself
on the field, you're actually on the field. See yourself as if
through a camera? No, see yourself from within, breaking
plays, tackling, picking up combinations, routes, coverages.
Example: Take each play and block it versus all defensive possibilities! Pass protect, protections vs. all rushes! Take each
defensive front vs. all runs. Take each coverage vs. all routes.
We've finished the physical preparation, now the mental
preparation begins. Mentally maximize your abilities (individuals). What will it take from me Saturday? Play hard! How
hard? Hit hard! How hard? Play smart! How tough? Every
game you ever play you make the decision how much effort
your make and how ready mentally you are going to be. Shoot
for the Personal Record, this way you're always improving!

Individuals. It's a team game but it's made up of individuals.
You want to help your team. Goal: I don't want to let them
down! Groups. Start thinking about building pride in your
group: Offense, defense, offensive line, defensive line, running
back, defensive backs. Help and support—make your group
best in the Pac-10. Use of the time, improve through mental
preparation. Cut back on the idle chatter from now on. Don't

entertain, respect the guy that is trying to get ready! Payback—War, now we put it all on the line, all of our hard work. Gain Texas A&M's respect. Kick ass.

The Huskies unveiled their new one-back offensive set and beat Texas A&M 19-6. Cary Conklin completed 23 of 37 passes for 224 yards, including a 22-yard, first-quarter scoring strike to Mario Bailey. John McCallum kicked four field goals for the Huskies, and Greg Lewis gained 133 yards on 29 carries.

A Technique for Visualizing Victory
September 6, 1990

In his Thursday speech, before the No. 20-ranked Huskies hosted San Jose State, James offers his most specific instructions on how the Huskies can use visualization to improve their game performance.

> Relaxation and Visualization. We all pretty well agree that after practice today you can't physically practice but you can and must use all available time practicing mentally through visualization. How do we do this? It's been proven that the best way is to totally relax your body and methodically play the game over and over in your mind. A couple of comments about relaxation. Your body must be relaxed for your mind to be receptive to the process. Since visualizations are so powerful, the more relaxed we are the more the subconscious believes the reality of the process.

> Relaxation: We are trying to balance training and rest. We want to rest and relax. We don't want you uptight for 48 hours. How do we do this? Breathing. Correct breathing is one of the most valuable techniques for calming, focusing, and energizing that an athlete can learn. Diaphragmatic (belly) breathing increases oxygen into the bloodstream and therefore increases the amount of oxygen to your muscles. Progressive relaxation—major muscle groups tense and relax. Long form—

breathe deep. Go from body limb to limb, relax. Short form—breathe deep. If you feel you can relax a portion of your body—do that muscle group.

Now visualization—two ways. See from within, most common, you view yourself actually doing it! A camera lens—you see yourself on the field as through you are watching videotape. Visualize yourself performing perfectly, well, great technique and form. You start in the huddle from the very beginning, you get the play or defense, you get the snap count, you see the opponent and you react successfully. You play the game over and over in your mind—runs, passes, kicks. Offense: Snap, block, run, catch, throw. Defense: Force runs, cover passes, stop tricks. Feel yourself totally relaxed, confident, and in complete control of your body and your mental state. Your subconscious must believe it's real! This is how we prepare ourselves to get top performances, our personal records, PRs.

During any free time, on the bus, in your hotel room, get your minds on the game, play it over and over, relax. Feel the tightness go—try the short form, breathe deep! So we all must cut back on idle chatter. We want to build on this up to kickoff on Saturday. This team, San Jose State, left our stadium thinking we were not very good in 1988 when we beat them 35-31. If there is no wind advantage, and we win the toss, we will take the ball. Let's demonstrate the Holy Shit Principle from the opening kickoff! Let's show them what the 1990 team is all about! Convincing offense, defense, kicking game.

It was not convincing, but the Huskies hung on to beat San Jose State 20-17. The teams were tied at 10 after three quarters before Mike Dodd kicked a 26-yard field goal and Beno Bryant returned a punt 52-yards for a touchdown to seal the Huskies' win.

Part III

GLIMMERS

Introduction

In the several interviews I conducted with Coach James, our topics strayed broadly into aspects of his career, his life, and his approach to leadership. These topics are developed in the following brief essays, or "glimmers," that provide greater insight into Don James the person and the coach.

Military Discipline

While attending the University of Miami during the Korean Conflict, James had joined the ROTC and served his two-year commitment after graduation with assignments in Virginia and New Orleans. Meantime, his former high school coach, Chuck Mather, had become head coach at the University of Kansas. James became a graduate assistant for Mather in the 1956-57 season, coaching the Jayhawks' freshmen—earning a master's degree in education in one year.

The military experience, especially the discipline, impressed him.

> That was good discipline. That's a regimented system, some-body says something and you do it [snaps his fingers] right now. I thought that was good training. And that's one thing I learned: When I said something, I want guys to listen, I want

them to react, to do things. It killed me when I would tell the team and tell the coaches I wanted this done this way and they went out and did something different. It's just like calling the play, without discipline you're not going off on the snap count. It's not going to work. It's just the same as the military.

For discipline to truly become ingrained in a team, James said it must be emphasized daily and practiced both on and off the field.

We know that when we play on Saturday afternoon we can't win unless we're disciplined. All the fans and the alumni expect us to be a disciplined team—to get out of the huddle, to get the play run, and not make a lot of mistakes. I've known that, but where people make mistakes is that to be disciplined on Saturday, you've got to be disciplined Sunday, Monday, Tuesday, Wednesday, Thursday and Friday.

Learning from Legends

With limited coaching opportunities available after his graduate assistantship at Kansas, Don and Carol James moved back to Miami. James joined the football staff for two years at Southwest Miami High School and taught math and physical education. Still, he longed to coach in college and wondered if he would get a chance. It was highly unusual for high school coaches to transition to the college ranks. Bob Breitenstein, who recruited James to Miami, knew Perry Moss, the new head coach at Florida State University, and urged him to hire James. James went to Tallahassee for an interview and Carol went to visit her folks at their winter home in Hollywood, Florida. Carol's folks had just arrived and their telephone was not yet working. So when James was hired, he couldn't share the news with her. She got the newspaper off the front porch and read that her husband had landed his first full-time college coaching job. The couple moved to Tallahassee on Feb. 14.

"Carol always said that was the best Valentine present she ever received," James said.

Moss left FSU for the Canadian Football League after Don's first year. Bill Peterson, from Louisiana State University, replaced Moss and James spent six seasons with him. Working for Peterson, James learned the philosophies of some of the greatest football coaches in history. The Southeast Conference was—and remains—an outstanding conference, and James became part of a storied coaching tree. He learned the thoughts and practices of coaching legends like Bobby Dodd and General Robert Neyland (considered one of the best defensive football coaches ever). He learned of Paul "Bear" Bryant's style of smash-mouth, tough play combined with superior quickness and speed. Peterson had learned firsthand from legends like Bryant, Colonel Earl Henry "Red" Blaik, and Sid Gillman, and he taught James everything he knew. Peterson had been offensive line coach for LSU head Coach Paul Dietzel and was on the staff of the 1958 LSU National Championship team. Dietzel had worked for Blaik, Gillman and Bryant and shared their wisdom with Peterson, who brought many of Dietzel's philosophies of program development to FSU in 1960. James, well known for his attention to detail and organization skills, credited much of that to the Bryant approach.

> I think we all adapted our off-season program philosophy to the quickness and intensity of the game as the Bear coached it. The idea was to get each young man to give you a 4- to 6-second sellout in all of our drill work. That would translate to doing the same on game day.

James spent his first few seasons as FSU's defensive backs coach before becoming the team's defensive coordinator (while coaching the secondary). In four seasons as defensive coordinator, the Seminoles recorded 13 shutouts, and held three other teams to one field goal and each of 14 other opponents to just a single touchdown. In his second to last year at FSU, James led a defense that was first in the nation in fumble recoveries, third against the rush, fifth in overall defense, seventh in scoring defense, and ninth in punt coverage. That team allowed only 75 yards a game on the ground, and knocked out 32 fumbles—recovering 23.

James' reputation as a defensive wizard was growing rapidly. In all of his football experience as a player and coach in high school and college, several things made indelible impressions on him and defined how he would approach being a head coach. He had experienced an alcoholic coach, a few mean coaches who verbally abused and swore at players, and coaches who "manhandled kids."

"They swore at them, grabbed their facemasks, beat the hell out of kids. I saw those things going on, which I didn't want any part of," he said.

"So then I go to Florida State and learn another approach. I see a very aggressive coaching staff, hard on kids, but off the field they were good to kids." James said he knew that's how he wanted to treat young men.

To Michigan, Then Colorado

After seven years at Florida State, James was approached by the University of Michigan's venerable head Coach Bump Elliott. Elliott had taken the Wolverines to the Rose Bowl the previous year but lost two assistants—his defensive coordinator and his secondary coach. James was hired to fill both vacancies in a program that won consistently but lagged behind the times in other ways, such as the number of assistants, the recruiting budget, and even the availability of film projectors.

When he arrived, James was surprised to find Michigan had fewer coaches than most Division I football programs in the nation. He spent only two seasons (1966 and 1967) at Michigan before an impending change of the school's athletic director, and rumored hiring of Bo Schembechler, made all the coaches' jobs uncertain. In what may have been a prescient move, James left Michigan to become the defensive coordinator for Eddie Crowder, head coach at Colorado. The next year, Bump Elliott finished 8-2 at Michigan but was released to make room for Schembechler.

The move from Ann Arbor to Boulder paid off. James enjoyed three great seasons at Colorado. Crowder, who sat at the feet of Coach Bud

Wilkinson at Oklahoma, taught James many things like how to identify a problem and address it with surgical precision without upsetting the entire team.

> In other words, if you were the problem on the defense, he would take it out on you and not on the team or the defense. He had the ability to identify the sores and heal the sores and I kind of appreciated that everybody didn't catch hell because we lost the game. And not that he would try to blame a player or blame a coach, but he'd try to figure out how to solve that problem so it didn't happen again.

James also learned much about player evaluation from Crowder, who dug deep into players' backgrounds to assess their character—an approach far more thorough than that of most coaches at that time.

"They did more of that, a better job of it, than anybody else I ever worked for," he said.

A Chance to Be Head Coach

Following Colorado's 17-3 loss to Tulane in the 1970 Liberty Bowl, James was approached by Kent State University in Ohio, which offered him his first opportunity to become a Division 1 head coach.

"Most everyone told me, 'Don't go. It's the graveyard of coaches.' But you don't get that many chances to become a head coach and I felt that Kent State could become a good football school, and that I could put together a staff that could win," James said.

James led the Golden Flashes to the 1972 Mid-American Conference Championship and a berth in the Tangerine Bowl against the Tampa Spartans. The Spartans coached by Earle Bruce—like James, an eventual College Hall of Fame member—won 21-18. Kent State players of note in the game included Nick Saban, head coach of Alabama, Missouri head Coach Gary Pinkel, and Pro Football Hall of Fame linebacker Jack Lambert. Tampa players in the game included John

Matuszak, selected by the Houston Oilers in 1973 as the NFL's No. 1 draft pick. In four years at Kent State, from 1971-1974, James compiled a 25-19-1 record and built a reputation as among the most promising young head coaches in the land.

The Leader as Role Model

Becoming a head coach for the first time was a big change for James.

"As an assistant coach, I was one kind of a personality," he said. "I was a lot more outgoing, I was a lot more enthusiastic, I was a lot more energetic on the practice field, I always worked my guys hard, and I ran the drills enthusiastically."

As a head coach, James said he believed it was important to temper his enthusiasm.

> When I became a head coach, I knew I had to calm down on the sideline. If I ever disintegrated under pressure, I gave all the players a chance to do so. If I did, if I screamed and threw clipboards and ranted and raved, that was their excuse then to do so. Plus, for decision-making, you've got to maintain some calm. So, from a leadership standpoint, I felt like, sure, I can get mad, I can say things, handling anger is probably one of the hardest things in the world for anybody. I didn't want to use too many four-letter words. I didn't want to embarrass myself. But you've got to work on all those things because you're going to get mad.

As a head coach, James saw his role as "coach of the coaches"—directing and correcting his assistants who, in turn, directed the players. In our interviews, James said a head coach sometimes must enforce consequences with assistants and model for them correct ways to motivate and communicate with players.

> It's like a parent. If you scream at them all day long and don't back it up, then they just don't listen to you. Every now and

then you have to put your foot down and say, "No John, that's it, that's not right, you go to your room." I felt that if I'm going to be the key communicator, I've got to be the model. If I'm going to be the key motivator, I've got to be the model.

Among his frequent admonishments to players and coaches alike was "Come to work early and stay late to improve." It was more than a slogan for James; he lived it.

"If I ask them to do that," James said, "then I've got to be there first, I've got to be around when everybody is gone." James learned his work ethic from his father, Thomas James, who worked two full-time jobs. No one outworked Don James.

James' 'Winning Edge': The Kicking Game

James told me that before his first season at Washington, he had read the book *The Winning Edge* by Miami Dolphins Coach Don Shula. Shula wrote the book the year after the Dolphins won an unprecedented 17 consecutive games, going undefeated en route to the Super Bowl in 1974.

Shula believed his winning edge was his conditioning program. Shula felt the "gassers," the drills the Dolphins did, made them the most highly conditioned team in the NFL.

"His point was that in any business to be successful you have to find some niche where you have a chance to have an edge. If you don't, someone is going to get you because someone is going to be better," James said.

As he began preparing for his first season at Washington in 1975, James surveyed the Huskies' talent pool and determined they would not win the Pacific-8 Conference on offense or defense. The kicking game, he felt, offered the Huskies their best and perhaps only chance to win the conference championship and go to the Rose Bowl.

James committed to the kicking game as his "winning edge" at Washington and soon demonstrated how it could shift momentum in games and create bedlam for opponents. He devoted valuable practice time to the kicking game, spending one-third of each practice on all aspects of kicking. James declared the special teams as important as the offense or defense.

His belief in the kicking game began paying major dividends in the final half of 1975.

"We moved (Robert) Spider Gaines (a world-class high hurdler) to blocking kicks and field goals and punts and he just drove everybody nuts," James said. "And then the kids started having fun, the kicking game, the special teams. Some of the seniors said 'this is more fun than we've had in four years.'"

The kicking game proved to be the great equalizer for Washington, buying James crucial time to build the program through outstanding recruiting resulting from his resurgent Husky football program.

> These teams' programs were ahead of us. The California schools had great talent back in those days, even better than we had, and the Oregons and Washington State they would play out of their heads against us so they equalized talent just because of the way they hated us and the way they prepared for us. I figured this was the way we could get an edge. And I believed in the kicking game.

As a former player and coach in the SEC, James learned a vastly different approach to kicking. He had seen coaches emphasize special teams and use them to great strategic advantage. Some coaches in the South even chose to punt on third down to catch the opponent off guard and put them in a hole. James never wanted to punt on third down, but he got a glimpse of how the kicking game could be his ace in the hole.

> I grew up in coaching in the Southeast and that's Bear Bryant's influence again. "The General," Robert Neyland, was at

Tennessee and Bobbie Dodd was at Georgia Tech. Those guys would punt on third down when they were backed up. It was ball control, kicking game, gain 10 yards on every drive and then get in and kick a field goal or get in the red zone (inside the 20 yard-line). They worked the kicking game. They would punt because they didn't want to screw up. They didn't want to throw an interception on third down. So I kind of grew up with that emphasis in the South in seven years at Florida State.

The kicking game card proved to be a real cool hand for James at Washington.

We won the first seven or eight years here because of the kicking game. We were underdogs most of the time and beat people through the kicking game. We just kicked their butts with punt returns and blocked kicks and we spent more time on it. We had to figure out a way to get an edge and that was the only way I could figure we were going to get an edge. We weren't going to be bigger, stronger, and faster than most of the people we played.

In 1975, James had his eye on Gaines, the lanky freshman wide receiver from Oakland, California, who was faster than just about everyone he played against. Gaines was on the scout team as a freshman, not playing varsity, and James got his stopwatch out during kicking drills, timing Spider as he was rushing the punter. James had a well-educated hunch that Gaines might be able to block some punts. He approached Gaines who said he wanted to give it a try. In the sixth game of the season, against Stanford, James unveiled his secret weapon.

"He blocked two punts in that one game and both of them were converted into touchdowns," James said. "He just drove people nuts from then on."

In a mere seven minutes of playing time the entire season, Gaines blocked a field goal against Oregon State—the week after Stanford—

deflected a field goal against UCLA the next week, and two weeks later trapped the USC punter for a safety in the end zone that lifted the Huskies to an 8-7 victory over the Trojans. Against Washington State, Gaines caught three TD passes, including a 78-yard strike on the final play of the game to lift the Huskies over the Cougars, 28-27. Gaines also advanced to finals of the Olympic Trials in 1976, and as a junior was rated No. 5 in the United States and eighth in the world as a 110-meter high hurdler.

The Huskies spent far more time on the kicking game than any of their opponents.

"By far more than anybody else. We had the specialty period before practice, and I didn't put it at the end, we inserted it in the middle. If it's in the middle then players mentally think, 'this is just as important as running our offense or defense.' A lot of coaches put it at the end and everybody is kind of tired. We gave it more emphasis, more time. It might not be one-third of the game in total snaps, but it's importance is one-third of the game," he said.

Not One for Beer with the Guys

Unlike many college football coaching staffs, James did not socialize with his assistants on Thursday nights or after games.

> I have never been one of the guys that stops on the way home from work to have a drink. The beer stuff and the men's night out, we were out enough with recruiting. A lot of staffs would go out Thursday night after practice and have some beer. I just never did. For me, it was get home and get on the phone recruiting and spend some time with my family. That was always the approach that I took. With all the nights that you work and are out and the one night that you can come home for dinner and you go out with the guys for beer? That just did not make sense to me. I don't think Carol would have been very happy had I not been that way.

Coaches Are Teachers

"Coaching is teaching, so coaches are teachers," James told me, explaining the importance he assigned to hiring good teachers. "I've had coaches who were very good teachers who were not in education who had other degrees, business degrees and other disciplines. In fact my receivers coach for a couple years there had a law degree."

He offered the example of a receivers coach teaching a player how to run a particular route.

"I've got to determine what it takes to run a route and run it effectively and teach you how to do it, and teach you the coverages and all the detail things and we can really help with that because we've got a lot of teaching aids. We've got the videotape, we've got overhead projectors, we've got blackboards," James said.

To ensure his coaches used sound teaching techniques, James had them present their lessons to him—before the players arrived in fall camp.

> If they are drawing plays and they've got stuff all over the board, I said "You're not going to be drawing a play up for the players, they are going to be looking at everything on that damn board. Get everything off of there except the play you're drawing." Some guys draw the plays upside down. If you're drawing offensively, you've got to draw it that way. Because I'm looking at it and I'm going up the board. If you are drawing defense, you've got to draw it coming down at me because I'm looking and I want to see how it's coming at me. And there are the little things, like "don't talk to the board, talk to the players." Everything I would see them do in meetings, I would say, "Hey, that's upside down. Get all that other crap off the board. I can't understand what you just said so how are those players going to understand it?"

> That happened every year, a guy would be going so fast that, I'd say "Now wait a minute, I'm a head coach, I have made a career of coaching. I don't have a clue what the hell you are

talking about. So those players are not going to understand what you are saying unless you back up and slow down." And that's a big part of communication, too, speaking at the level of your group. There's a guy who is an experienced coach and he is speaking over my head and not doing a good job. Now if he's got a freshman in there, you'd better be good at communicating and teaching at the level that those kids are on. Transmit and receive information clearly, they say. We also as coaches know a million plays. That playbook is so thick, but we can't teach all of those plays. We've got to take out the key six runs this week and the key four or five passes and have a draw and a screen. That's part of teaching too, knowing how much can they absorb within the time they have.

With his background as a teacher, James realized that players learned in different ways. While some could pick up concepts easily from a playbook or a chalkboard, others needed to see videotape to learn best, and still others learned best by going through a play on the field to experience it physically.

That's why we always wanted to hand them the playbooks so they could see it, we wanted to lecture to them on the board, show them a videotape of it, and then get out and do it. And then, film it, and critique it. You know the trigger comes in different areas. Some guys can read the book and pick it up, other guys say "that didn't make any sense. I partly understood it when he was drawing it up, but when I saw it on video and how it was supposed to work and I've really got the idea; now I've just got to go out and do it."

All Ideas Sought, Valued

Don James had seen some head coaches fail because they refused to recognize the power of ideas from others. For this reason, he required all assistants to provide a game plan.

"I'd go to them on the weekend right before they are starting on their game plan and I would say: 'I want every assistant to come up with a plan.' I didn't want eight guys loafing and expecting the defensive and offensive coordinators and myself to come up with all the ideas," James said. "I wanted everybody to have ideas. If Skip Hall is coaching the outside linebackers, I want Skip to come up with a defensive plan. I want his ideas, that's one of the advantages you get."

James said there is a name for the failure by a head coach to use others' ideas: "dominant leadership"—a phenomenon he had witnessed as an assistant.

> I've seen head coaches who do everything. You just lose eight or nine guys' ideas. If you've got four guys on offense and four on defense and two or three of them are not even thinking or are relying on someone else, you've just lost a lot of good ideas. I wanted a game plan from everybody. I'd get in on the offensive side and say to the running backs coach, "OK, what do you think we ought to do?" To the receivers coach, I'd say, "What do you think we ought to do? What do we have to do to pick up this offense? We're not moving the ball, we're having trouble." Some guys have got more plays and some guys have more simple ideas.

After gathering all of the ideas from the other coaches, James would step up to provide the final direction, which typically included ideas from many others.

> I'd say "OK, now these are my ideas. With all these ideas, this is the direction I want to see us go." I'd leave and let them hammer it out.

Leading from the Tower

From the beginning at Washington, James viewed most practices not by walking around the field but from a 60-foot-high perch atop a scaffolding erected near the 50 yard line. James would typically walk around on the field during stretching and the individual and group drills and ascend the tower when any team drills or scrimmages began. His reasons for doing so were purely practical.

> If you get to be a head coach, it's because you've probably had some success in a particular area. In other words, you were an offensive coordinator or a defensive coordinator. Then as you step into that next role, you've got to make a decision: "Am I going to continue coordinating what I had been coordinating as an assistant?" As an assistant coach, I felt like every time the head coach came and coached my guys, it made me look bad. It made me look like I was not worth it, or that I wasn't doing the job because he's got to coach my guys. And it's not like he can't come by and see something and improve on it. It wasn't that, but if he takes over my segment of the game it does make me look bad.

> The other point is if the head coach coordinates the offense or the defense or the kicking game, then he can't see what's going on all over the field. He might have a coach down there just kicking a guy right in the rear end, that will get you all fired, but he can't see it if he's up there coordinating at the other end of the field. I didn't have an ego that I needed to be out there coordinating something, or calling everything. Number two, I felt I could get more productivity out of my coaches if I let them coach on the field and, three, I felt I could make more good decisions by seeing everything from the tower.

The tower view also led to some decisions with immediate impact.

"I made personnel decisions that I never mentioned to anybody that were so successful," he said, such as the case of Jacque Robinson.

The scout squads, comprised mostly of freshmen that don't play on varsity, imitate the upcoming opponent's offense and defense each week. In 1981, before the Huskies played USC, Robinson, a freshman, was doing an outstanding job of imitating USC tailback Marcus Allen.

"I went to our staff meeting the next morning and said, 'Hey, our freshman running back is looking better than anybody we've got on the other end of the field with our offense.'"

Robinson was suddenly moved up to varsity, played a role in Washington's victory over USC, played well the following week against Washington State University, and became the Most Valuable Player in the Huskies' Rose Bowl victory over Iowa that season.

"You can't make those kind of decisions if you're down on the field, focused on one side of the ball," James said.

Bear Bryant was among the first and most well known of the coaches to use a tower in practice.

Since he had always videotaped the Huskies' practices, James' observations from the tower, supported by his notes and the practice video, created a critical mass of data that he used to better evaluate players and critique assistant coaches. James took lots of notes in practice to share with his assistants to make sure problems were addressed at every position.

Delegating the coordination of the offense and the defense freed James to literally see the big picture, and allowed him to make crucial strategic decisions.

> Egowise, I didn't need to be out there taking over. It satisfied me. And the older I got, when it started raining it was good to have something over your head and I put walls up on the side and kept the wind out. I think there were some players who probably felt I was a little standoffish because I wasn't out there around them. You can see a heck of a lot from that tower. You can see at both ends. Everything is scripted so I knew exactly what play was coming up at both ends of the

field. I knew what the scout team was running and I knew what the offense was running. I could really look for things. I might take one 20-minute period and really zero in on this phase of the offense, and another 20- or 30-minute period I might zero in on the defense.

Joe Steele recalled an incident in his sophomore season, 1977, involving James on the tower and Al Roberts, who was in his first season as the Huskies' running backs coach from Seattle's Garfield High School.

"Al was a little on edge all the time just coming in his first year as a coach from Garfield High. Don would be up in his tower and he could see the whole field. No matter where you were on the field, everyone thought Don was looking at them. Neither player nor coach liked to be called over to the tower for a comment from D.J. Al got called over during a practice. When Al returned, he pulled me aside and said, 'in the last drill, you were carrying the ball in the wrong arm.' Al let me have it a little bit. In the future I made darn sure that I was carrying the ball in the proper arm. Don's attention to detail was incredible and was always intended to eliminate mistakes and make us the best we could be," Steele said.

Creativity a Hallmark of James' Career

Creativity played an important role in James' coaching, even as an assistant.

"I tried to think of things and do things to stop people that no one else had ever done," he said. One innovation, which he came up with as an assistant at Florida State, was the idea of combination coverages on defense in which two defenders would combine to cover two receivers, depending on their routes.

I'm (the defender) going to roll to the side of the route. Maybe I'm going to have it deep and you are going to have it short.

We don't know who is going deep and who is going short, so we are just going to settle off and pick off the combination. We called it "banjo" for linebackers. The inside linebacker and the outside linebacker would key on that tailback, if he came in here you've got him, if he came out there, you've got him.

James said the plan helped the Seminoles beat Miami when he was an FSU assistant.

James developed another key innovation, the "5-under, 2-deep" defensive coverage. In it, two players covered the deep half zones of the field while five other players covered the underneath zones, aggressively hitting the receivers as rules allowed.

Toward the end of his tenure at FSU, James asked LSU Defensive Coordinator Bill Beals if he had any ideas about defending Baylor, which spread the field well and threw the ball. James took the basic idea from Beals, refined it, and deployed it to help beat Baylor.

As the defensive coordinator at Michigan, James kept his little-known defensive scheme close to the vest until he needed it most: to stop passing phenomenon and future NFL Hall of Fame quarterback Bob Griese of Purdue, who was racking up massive passing yardage against his befuddled opponents.

"We held him to 63 yards and shut him down," James said. His secret was out.

> That year, Purdue won the [Big Ten Conference] championship and went to the Rose Bowl and [then-USC head coach] John McKay called [then-Michigan head coach] Bump Elliott and said "I see this coverage. I've never seen it before." My office was right outside and he says, "Well, I'll get Don in here." So I spent 30-40 minutes giving it to John McKay to use in the Rose Bowl, 5-under, 2-deep. And in John McKay's book he says, "Yeah we were preparing for Purdue in the Rose Bowl and as I was walking through campus and like a bolt of lightning it struck me and hit me in the head and I thought of this

5 under coverage with 2 deep." He took the credit for it. I got the original idea from LSU. But that was funny.

After Michigan, when James was the defensive coordinator at Colorado, he interviewed for a coaching position with the Oakland Raiders. Then-Raiders' head Coach John Madden had heard about the coverage James had developed.

> He had me go to the board in front of the whole staff and I put it out and went through it. He said, "It will never work. In the pros you can't cover all that territory with two guys." And that's been their lifeblood for the last 20 years. The 2-deep, 5-under and variations of it. But that was fun to be a part of stuff like that.

As a defensive coordinator, James also came up with the idea of attaching a 1-inch-wide strip on the left-hand side of the scouting report page that lists down and distances possibilities from the opponents' goal line all the way down the field to the Huskies' goal line. The sheet lists and charts opponents' tendencies for various plays and offensive sets and schemes at any spot on the field and virtually any down and distance to go for a first down.

> So we can go into the field on second and average and go to the plus 35-yard-line and find out every play you (the opponents) have run (in their previous games that season or, if it's an early season opponent, their tendencies in games the previous year) so we know what your tendencies are. I could first go across the top of that page and on every down, first through four, in any situation, and find out exactly what you would run. When you were really backed up, I'm going to find out how conservative you are. Will you throw the ball or will you just run off tackle? Conversely, I can come down to the goal-line and find out what you would run inside the 10 on every down, first and 10, second and long, second and average, second and short, third and long, average and short, fourth down.

Innovation Powers Huskies to Orange Bowl Victory

The Huskies finished the 1984 regular season 10-1, losing only to USC, and beating Oklahoma 28-17 in the Orange Bowl on New Year's Day in 1985. Knowing the benefits of innovative thinking, James encouraged his assistants to get creative with their game plan, considering they faced an immovable object in the Sooners' All American defensive lineman Tony Casillas, who went on to a long NFL career. Husky offensive assistant Dan Dorazio came up with a stroke of brilliance to block Casillas.

Called a "trapcheck," the play used Casillas' devastating strength and acceleration against him by employing a scheme involving double-team block and a classic trap. It worked beautifully, James said.

> Half the time we went in the huddle and we called the formation and called "trap check." Nobody could block Tony Casillas, so we'd double-team him and trap the next guy out and just run (running back) Rick Fenney up there. If he moved over to the guard, we would center back on the weakside tackle and put the right guard back on the linebacker and trap Tony Casillas. And we ran the old counter-trap with Jacque Robinson up there and we just killed them with those two plays. We were never wrong. All we did in the huddle was say "trap check" and when we'd get out there and could see where he (Casillas) was, we'd call the appropriate trap. There was no way one of our guys could block him, but we knew he was either going to be over center or over our right guard. We didn't worry about the linebacker, Brian Bosworth (James chuckles). Those are things that you do because you have to do them to have a chance to succeed.

Evaluating Personnel

All college football coaches realize that their teams can only be as good as the student-athletes they recruit. Coaches realize that no matter how talented they are at developing, motivating, and cajoling every drop of effort and energy from their student-athletes, the players' potential is generally limited to their size, speed, quickness, and natural athleticism. Recruiting new student-athletes, perhaps the single most important responsibility outside of on-field coaching, took place year-round and involved all coaches—each with his own geographic area of responsibility.

Upon arriving at Washington, James compiled a recruiting manual to help evaluate potential student-athletes, and he made sure every assistant coach followed it. James also employed the general recruitment philosophy that he used for players to hire coaches and office staff. His recruitment philosophies were highly effective, albeit never 100 percent accurate.

> I wanted everybody to use the evaluation system. I never believed in changing it. I thought it was good and it was effective. A high percentage of the kids we recruited had the ability to play if they would stick it out. I thought it was pretty thorough.

After having watched a prospect play, James' evaluation process consisted of 10 questions.

> Everybody has got their ideas about personnel. Some people use a test. I just had a series of questions. The first one is "can he be a great player?" We're asking his coach and two other people who played against him or who know him. And if I'm recruiting a coach, with the contacts I'm using, my references, I'll ask, "Can he be a great coach?"

The second question goes to a prospect's desire: "Is he dying to be a great player or coach?"

> So you open that up a little bit, there's a lot of guys with talent out there who don't get it done just because it's not that important to them. "Will he come early and stay late to improve?" That was always a question. Clock-watchers don't

get it done. If we say, "You need to be in the weight room 40 minutes to do this program." Well, you'll get stronger and it'll be good, but if you spent an hour and 10 minutes it will probably be better. Our minimum requirements we want everybody to handle; we're looking for guys that will get out there a little bit early and stay a little bit later.

The next question was: "Will he play any position to help the team win?"

We've got to move people around. I can't plug a coach into one position and expect that is the best when I find out he can do something better; I've got to move him. That was a good question because you get the player who says, "If I don't get to play tailback, I'm not going to play." Well you've got to go out and recruit eight tailbacks and move a couple to cornerback and a couple to receiver. As high school coaches, where are they going to put their best players? Tailback!

Other questions dealt with prospects' leadership abilities and their general character.

Players we had problems with, people lied to us. They were poor character guys, their coaches knew about it and they just lied to us. If you bring in a guy with poor character you fight them every day. They are into something every single day.

Questions dealing with injury and illness were among the other topics James used to evaluate personnel. James also dug into prospects' background to find out if they were tough enough, mentally and physically, not only to endure but to flourish.

The idea with mental toughness is that successful people are able to access their talent on demand, and if you are mentally tough, you do that. If you've got a cold or your shoulder hurts or your ankle hurts or you've got a little fever but you've still got to play the game; the game is played. Or if you are hurting out there on the field and it's third down-and-long and some-body runs a play at you—even if you're hurting—if you are mentally tough you will get the play stopped.

The final question James or his staff would ask about a prospective player or coach was, "When can this particular person contribute?" James wanted players and coaches to step in and contribute signifi-cantly immediately.

"It's like any business, how long can you pay somebody a salary before they start contributing?"

James said he decided as an assistant that when he became a head coach he would have the entire staff vote on whether to recruit a player, so accountability for recruiting would be shared by the entire staff. As an assistant, it irked him when nine coaches would go on the road recruiting and bring in whomever they felt could play without consent or approval from the rest of the staff.

> That always bothered me because if you get nine guys and four of them are poor recruiters, poor evaluators, then four guys are bringing in guys who can't play. I knew that when I became a head coach I didn't want nine guys going out and doing their own thing, that we were going to have a system and we were all going to use the system in evaluation.

Before any player was offered a scholarship at the University of Wash-ington, the entire staff would look at film of that recruit and each coach would vote on a scale of 1-4, denoting when he felt the player would be able to play at Washington. For instance, a player who re-ceived an overall grade from the Washington staff of 1.1 meant the staff felt he could play in the first game his first year, while the staff felt a player who received a grade of 3.1 could not play until the first game of his third year. Any player with a grade of 3.1 or higher would not be offered a scholarship.

> We were trying to get everybody involved so if a player comes in and doesn't play, we all had a chance to reject him,

we all sat in the meeting. That way five guys aren't upset with four guys because they are bringing in all the guys who couldn't play.

Some guys would go on the road and play around. I can go into any school in the world and find all the guys I want to give scholarships to. I can go in and find a big, good-looking guy who can't play a lick and give him a scholarship. And they're easy to recruit, those guys, nobody else wants them.

Heart, James said, can make up for some lack of natural talent, whereas raw natural talent alone is not enough to succeed.

There are some guys that had all the talent in the world, but there was just some spark missing, that heart to excel. And then there were guys that played a lot better that had that (heart) more so than talent, but they succeeded because it was so doggone important to them.

Jack Lambert, for example, weighed 184 pounds as a freshman at Kent State, where James coached the eventual Pittsburgh Steelers All-Pro and Pro Football Hall of Fame member.

You couldn't measure his heart. He weighed 204 in his first Super Bowl, still way underweight, way undersized, but just like a snake, a rattlesnake the way he would strike. It was just so important to him. Everybody turned down Jack Lambert. He walked on at Kent State and got a scholarship.

Paul Skansi, one of the Huskies' all-time receiving leaders, who also played nine years in the NFL, escaped the notice of most college recruiters as well. James saw him play in a high school all-star game and went after him.

It was us and UPS (University of Puget Sound) recruiting Skansi. The thing we would do is go watch him play basketball because we couldn't decide what to do. He was a good athlete, he didn't look real quick or fast, and we didn't have a 40 (yard dash) time. But we really liked his maneuverability and his hands. And his first day on the field up here there was no question he had big-time hands.

Always a Focus on Positive Coaching

In addition to his efforts to get players to use visualization during the final 48 hours before each game, James' focus on the mental aspects of football extended into how he wanted the Huskies to be treated. He frowned on berating or belittling players, and never tolerated that kind of behavior from his assistants. On those rare occasions when an assistant bullied or berated a player, James stepped in.

When necessary, James never backed away from sternly correcting assistants.

> If it was something that a coach was doing in my opinion that was wrong or incorrect—it could be a lot of different things. I did it in a way that they just knew it was coming. It could be swearing at a player. It could be grabbing their facemask. We're not going to grab facemasks, we're not going to lay a hand on a player. We're not going to be negative. We're not going to be telling players how bad they are. We are trying to build guys up, not tear them down. We're going to be positive.

When it came time to correct mistakes made during games, James said he learned early in his career that it was better to wait until the day after games to confront his assistants.

> I'd be so mad at an assistant coach, I couldn't wait to get off the field. I would get him in a shower or the locker room and I learned early that was not the best thing because the next morning I felt a lot differently about it. I always did a lot better job of critiquing with a night's sleep on it. I stopped getting mad in the shower and they appreciated that.

Playbook Basics

At the start of fall camp, coaches handed each new football player his own personal Husky football playbook. The playbooks were our year-round guides to most any questions we might have about the program or our position. Coach James reviewed the playbooks with all of his players in a group meeting. James' talent for organizational detail was stamped all over the playbooks, which contained both position-specific information—such as plays and techniques—and a section for all players with rules and guidelines on everything from emergency procedures to weight-room schedules to practice times, injuries, gambling, media relations, parking, dormitory security, laundry, and game tickets—to name a few. Nothing was left to chance.

> General Rules
>
> "The following general rules are for your benefit. Since it is impossible to cover every point or eventuality in a statement of team policy such as this, you are expected to conduct yourself at all times in a manner that will reflect credit upon you, your teammates, the football program, and the University of Washington."

The first section provides even more specific clarity on personal behavior.

> General:
>
> a. Work to improve language. Eliminate swearing, obscene words.
>
> b. Training rules: Live clean, think clean; tobacco, alcohol, and drugs are prohibited.
>
> c. Treat service personnel with respect. Make their job a pleasant experience.
>
> d. Girlfriends and wives are not permitted in rooms, fall camp, pre-game or training room.
>
> e. Arrests and criminal charges could result in suspension from the team. Conviction could result in loss of scholarship.

Near the front of the general section in the playbook, James lists the "Five Major Ingredients for Squad Development" as they appeared in the playbook (1992). He credited some of these to former Notre Dame Coach Lou Holtz.

1. HUSTLE
Not every man can start or make All-American, but everyone can hustle 100% of the time.

2. SHOW COURAGE
Football is like life, you get knocked down quite often. You have to keep getting up with a more determined effort to be successful. (Show of courage is the primary way to get your teammates' respect.) The more honor and respect among the team, the greater the team. Achievement is man's gift to God. There is no way we can win without having great respect for one another.

3. KNOW ASSIGNMENTS
There have been great players who have been deaf, but never one who was dumb. You can not be a successful player if you blow assignments. Must achieve consistency in order to be great.

4. CARE ABOUT WINNING
All great organizations are marked by a desire to achieve. Nothing can compare with the thrill of a team all pulling together for one common goal of winning. (If a player makes All-Conference, that doesn't make football a worthwhile endeavor for the third-stringer. Winning as a team is what makes football worthwhile. Everybody on the team must contribute to winning.)

5. LOYALTY
If we remain strong from within nothing from the outside can divide us. (Loyalty is something that must be practiced and preached if you want a sound program. Loyalty is defending anybody or anything that comes under attack by anyone.)

Part IV

A LASTING LEGACY

Introduction

Don James' legacy as one of America's greatest college football coaches of all time is secure, as Seattle sports journalist Steve Rudman wrote after the Oct. 27, 2013, memorial service for James. Hundreds of former players, coaches, fans and other admirers attended the service in the Alaska Airlines Arena at the University of Washington.

> Along the way, he out-coached the most acclaimed mentors of his day—Bo Schembechler, Hayden Fry, Bobby Bowden, Joe Paterno—and probably would have coached another decade if Pac-10 sanctions against his program, sanctions he believed unfair, hadn't prompted his resignation days before the start of the 1993 season. — *Steve Rudman*

Mike Lude, James' longtime friend and his athletic director at Kent State and the UW, might have best described James' legacy:

"He is the man who established the standard and tradition for all Husky coaches—now and for the future."

Michael Jackson, a star linebacker for the Huskies on the 1978 Rose Bowl team and an NFL player, said James was a larger-than-life figure.

"He was so generous. He was so loving. He was so *mean*. He was so little. He was so *big*, to this kid from Pasco (Washington)," Jackson said. "He is still looking over us," Jackson told the memorial service crowd. "So you'd better watch out!"

Coach Don James poses with the 1991 National Championship trophy after leading the Huskies to a 12-0 record and a Rose Bowl victory over Michigan.   *UW Photo*

Coach Gary Pinkel, University of Missouri

Gary Pinkel, head coach at the University of Missouri, played for James at Kent State and coached with him as a graduate assistant there and as an assistant coach at Washington. At the memorial, Pinkel said words fail to adequately describe the impact James had on his life.

> I met him when I was 18 years old. He had a profound impact on my life. Coach James was a huge influence in my life, personally and professionally; I wanted to coach because of Don James. He was my idol. He was my mentor. The values he taught included hard work, ethics, determination, perseverance, integrity, teamwork, and he was one of the most successful men with the most humility that I've ever met in my life. There were invaluable lessons that applied to my life when coaching kids for the last 36 years.

Pinkel was head coach at the University of Toledo before moving on to Missouri.

> The program we built at Toledo and the program we built at the University of Missouri is the Don James program. I have responsibility to pass on his coaching legacy. The foundation of Don James' program is meticulous organization, discipline, you play like you practice, and attention to detail. Coach was big on the (final) 48 hours of preparation. When that Thursday practice was over, we didn't practice on Friday, we played Saturday and we had 48 hours locked in.

Pinkel said James was one of the three most important men in his life—his father and his high school coach being the other two.

> Coach James was so important to me and my wife that in Waco, Texas, at the American Football Coaches Association home office they have what they call the Plaza of Influence. There is a big stone plaque there that I had made in his honor that says "Don James, Great Coach, Great Teacher, and Great Role Model. You Made a Difference in My Life."

Pinkel said he left a message for Coach James weeks before he died.

> It was very emotional because I didn't know if I would talk to him again. A week later, my secretary walked into my office and said, "Coach James is on the phone." I got to talk to him. I got to tell him thanks for all he did for me and the thousands of other people he touched. I got to tell him that I loved him. I will be so thankful for that phone call for the rest of my life. Coach James' influence and spirit will live forever.

Pinkel then read a poem, written by former Baylor football Coach Grant Teaff, titled *A Coach's Influence*.

In concluding, Pinkel said, "Coach James' influence continues. I love you coach."

Coach Nick Saban, University of Alabama

Nick Saban, head coach at the University of Alabama and a player and graduate assistant coach for James at Kent State, also spoke at the memorial service via a taped presentation.

> Coach James was my coach, my mentor, and my friend and there probably isn't anyone who influenced my life more than he did because of his leadership and the example that he set but also professionally as a coach. Our program today still reflects many of the things that we did and that I learned from Coach James when I first got into this profession, which he inspired me to get into this profession by asking me to be his graduate assistant at Kent State 40 years ago.

Saban said he didn't know what James saw in him, but said he can never have enough appreciation for James helping him get into a profession that he loves and in which he has become so successful.

> There is really only one word that I can come up with to describe Coach James and that's "class." There is nobody that I

look up to more because of how he cared about people. He was concerned that you were successful personally and that you would be more successful in life because you were involved in the program, and individual character development, academic success, how you competed as a football player—all of those things would contribute to that.

Saban added that Coach James' spirit lives through the many people whose lives he touched and changed.

"The lessons that we learned, the leadership that he provided, and the influence that he had impacted all of our lives tremendously," Saban said. "It was certainly a privilege to know this great man."

Sam Wick, Friend

Sam Wick, a longtime friend of Coach James, summed up James' priorities.

"Don was about faith, family, friends, and football," Wick said at the memorial service.

It's an honor for me to be called one of Don's friends. Our friendship has spanned more than 25 years and Don became like my brother. He truly was my very best friend. We talked or saw each other regularly for many years—building our homes in Palm Desert, right next to each other.

A devoted friend, Wick said he had been with James every day since Labor Day of 2013 when he became sick and was hospitalized.

"He was caring about all of his friends, even in spite of his pain and what he was going through," said Wick who never played or coached football. "We first met Don and Carol at church and started a deep friendship there. Don was a little better golfer than I was, but he would never give me strokes."

Among the qualities Wick said he admired most in James was his faith, which impacted his entire approach to life, and his humility.

"He had an active prayer list and he prayed every day for people he knew that needed prayer," Wick said, adding that James planned his own memorial ceremony and even had the singers at his home to rehearse before he died.

> We had Communion together and we had these songs. He was directing how it was going to go. Don was a very compassionate person. He was a very tenderhearted person and rarely said a bad thing about anyone. He was quick to forgive. He was a very emotional guy. He would easily be caught crying at a movie and even at a commercial and definitely over a few football games.

James, who was punctual to a fault, struggled with patience, Wick said.

"He was extremely sick and they were supposed to come for a surgical procedure at 1:45. We're waiting around and it was 2 o'clock and Don was not a happy camper. 'Carol, Carol go out and see where they are at.' When they did come he was saying they were late and he didn't know if he wanted to do it that day," Wick said. "Don had a favorite flower. He would say, 'Carol what's the name of that flower?' Carol would say, 'Remember what you always get?' 'Oh yeah, impatiens.'"

> Don said he would be laying down these trophies "because they will not be going with me to Heaven. They are just material things that Carol will get to dust." Instead, his lifelong trophies and crowns are his family and the thousands of lives that Don impacted and changed through his example of character and integrity in which he lived.

In closing, Wick said, "Don had that same integrity and character as he knew he was dying right to the end and he knew the Lord was waiting for him with open arms."

Jeffrey James, Grandson

James' grandson Jeffrey James also spoke at his memorial service. He recalled how in the weeks before his death, all of the grandchildren had the opportunity to write letters to him, expressing their love and the impact he had had on their lives.

> He always made it a priority to come to as many sporting events as he could and has or will send all 10 grandchildren through college. He was a role model. He showed us the importance of punctuality. He stressed faith by sending all the grandchildren letters this past Christmas by saying the greatest gift we could give him was accepting the Lord Jesus Christ as our personal savior. Instead of a Christmas present, all he wanted was each of us to have a personal relationship with Jesus.

Rev. Jerry Mitchell, Pastor at Crossroads Bible Church

Rev. Jerry Mitchell, the James family pastor at Crossroads Bible Church for 30 years, baptized Don in the Jordan River and went to Israel with Don and Carol. Rev. Mitchell said he celebrated Communion with Don before he died and they discussed what the pastor would say at his memorial service.

> He said, "There's going to be a lot of good things said about me by a number of different people, so pastor, I want you to tell them about my savior and I want them to know where I am and I want them to know how they can get there."

James invited the Lord into his life as a young coach when he wasn't doing well, the pastor said.

> He closed the door in his office and he got down on his knees and he said, "Lord, I turn over everything to you, everything I am, everything I will be, everything I've done, everything I will do—it all belongs to you." From that day forward, Don was a changed man because Jesus Christ invaded his life and gave

him direction. He was one of the finest men I've ever known. But what we don't often realize is that there is something going on on the inside, something very special, a faith that is very real that changed Don and helped form him into the man that many of us came to respect.

Jill Woodruff, Daughter

Jill Woodruff is one of Don and Carol's three children. The others are Jeff and Jeni. Jill said "legacy" was a word she heard frequently in the waning months of her father's life.

> The legacies that we, his family, believe are truly his finest, go hand-in-hand with the priorities my father lived by. The No. 1 priority in his life was his relationship with God. Over the last 40 years he made it his goal to read through the Bible every year. And not only did he read through the Bible, he tried to live by its principles.

Jill said her father's next most important priority was his relationship with her mother, Carol, Don's bride of 61 years. She shared a story of the time, during her father's critical third year of a four-year contract at Washington, when her mother drove to his office one day.

> She closed the door behind her and told my dad she kind of felt like he was putting his job before she and the kids. He got out from behind his big oak desk and put his arms around her and said, "I will resign, effective today, if that's what I need to do because nothing will ever come before you and the family."

Jill added that her father's relationships with his children rounded out his top priorities—each one more important to him than football.

> My dad worked incredibly long hours, but when he had time off he came home and spent his time with us and we never doubted where we stood on the priority list of his life. These are the legacies we will cherish as his family.

Jill said her father accepted the last and greatest challenge of his life by fighting pancreatic cancer in the same dignified and systematic manner that he approached all others.

> He gathered information, weighed his options and formulated a game plan. The plan had to be adjusted, tweaked, and each day played itself out. Then the day came when my dad, the ultimate competitor, knew it was time to take a knee—as they say in the game of football—and he surrendered to God's final game plan for his life.

In her father's waning hours, his family gathered by his bedside in prayer. Jill recalls she was reading from the Psalms before her brother, Jeff, said "Jill, read John:11:25," a verse that was included in the memorial program.

"So I turned to the Book of John and read these words that Jesus spoke: 'I am the resurrection and the life. He who believes in me will live even though he dies,'" Jill told the memorial service crowd. "No sooner had those words left my mouth than my dad leaned forward in bed and took his last breath."

The family members all looked at their watches and, remarkably, the time was exactly 11:25 a.m.

"This verse we will forever treasure as a family, and I will look forward to the day when I can read it by my daddy's side again in Heaven," Jill said. Later that night, Jill reflected on the day's events and began to smile.

> In those last seconds, God had somehow encapsulated everything that my dad was, lived for, and believed in for he truly believes that Jesus was the resurrection and the life. He lived for his family who were all by his bedside that morning and it encompassed one of my father's greatest attributes—his impeccable talent for time management and attention to detail. That was quite a gift, and he was quite a dad. I love you, Dad.

Made in the USA
Lexington, KY
31 January 2015